Positive Psychology

for a successful life

Dr.Y. Narasimha Raja

Ph.D., MBA, M.Sc. Psychology

Asst. Professor –School of Management,
Presidency University, Bengaluru

Email: ynraja.phd@gmail.com
Web: www.ynraja.com
Mob: +(91)8073205840

Copyrights Certification @ 2024
Positive Psychology for a Successful life
Dr. Y. Narasimha Raja & All rights reserved

MRP: Indian Rupees (INR) 250/-

PublishersDr. Y. Narasimha Raja
297, Raja Nivas, 11th Main, 11th cross, Narasipura Layout,
Vidyaranyapura, Bengaluru -560097
Ynraja;phd@gmail.com, www.ynraja.com
Mob: +91-8073205840

Contents

Preface

"Desire changes nothing, Decision changes something, But Determination of Positive thought changes everything. Success starts with every challenges, not from the comfort zone. There no "right time " in life, there is just time and you get to choose what to do with in.

This quote has inspired the author to keep their maximum efforts to write this book.This book is your guide to becoming a champion in leading a positive psychological thought process.

This book is emphasized modern concepts of happiness, stop overthinking,emotional intelligence, positive mindset,character strengths,well-being, interpersonal relationships,flow / engagement, optimism, resilience, meaning,accomplishments, gratitude, hope.

This book provides a broad range of information concisely and in an easy-to-read manner. I assure you that if these principles are applied to your practical life situations, you will see positive results in a short span of time.

Written in simple language and self-explanatory, this book aims to empower readers.

With you and for you

Dr. Y. Narasimha Raja

About Author

Dr. Y. Narasimha Raja multifaceted professional with significant contributions to the fields of psychology, management, and human resources. His extensive educational background, with a Ph.D. in Management Studies and multiple master's degrees, complements his over 19 years of experience in corporate and academic sectors across India and internationally. As an award-winning HR practitioner and corporate trainer, Dr. Raja's expertise has been recognized by numerous prestigious awards and certifications.

Book Publications

1. Highly Effective Parenting Skills
2. Highly Effective Teaching Skills
3. The best & smart Teaching techniques
4. Happy Parenting Skills
5. Stage Fear – 101 Techniques to overcome the stage fear.
6. Highly effective Public Speaking Skills
7. Phobias-Overview on 165 phobias
8. Neuro Disorders
9. Counseling Skills
10. How to change life better?
11. Positive Psychology for a Successful people.

Chapter-1

Life value of Positive Psychology (PERMA+)

*The difference between an obstacle and an opportunity
is our attitude towards it. Every opportunity has a
difficulty, and every difficulty has an opportunity"*
J Sidlo Baxter

When we fail to understand the **lessons** at the **right time**, life makes us understand the **same lessons** at the **wrong time**. Opportunities are never lost; they are always taken by the people who are ready. We should understand the value of **positive psychology** at all times.

Positive Psychology in difficult times

"It was a rough weather & rainy day, the airplane was flying high up in the sky, heading towards its destination. Suddenly, the airplane face the turbulence. The air hostess quickly announced for everyone to tighten their seat belts. They stopped serving drinks to the passengers because the turbulence was very strong. Among the passengers were businessmen, celebrities, and many others. Everyone started to feel panicked because it seemed like something serious was happening with the plane.

As the turbulence got worse, the plane shook more and more. In the midst of the panic, there was a young boy sitting calmly, reading his comic book. He had a peaceful smile on his face, unlike the rest of the passengers who were worried. Eventually, the plane made an emergency landing. Thankfully, it was a safe landing, and no one was hurt.

One of the passengers sitting next to the boy was curious and asked him, "Dear brave boy, how were you able to stay so calm during the turbulence and not look surprised after the safe landing?" The boy replied, "The person piloting the flight is my father. I trust my father completely. I know he would never put me in danger. So, when my beloved father is flying the plane, why should I be worried? He knows how to keep me safe better than anyone else."

The moral of the story is about "Positive Psychology" hope and confidence in one's father. The boy's unwavering positive trust in his father's abilities gave him the strength to remain calm even in a stressful situation. It teaches us that having faith in our loved ones can help us navigate through difficult times with courage and peace of mind.

Origion of Positive Psychology :-

Positive psychology is a branch of psychology that focuses on the scientific study of human well-being, happiness, and the factors that contribute to a fulfilling and meaningful life. Unlike traditional psychology, which often emphasizes the diagnosis and treatment of mental illnesses and disorders, positive psychology seeks to understand what makes life worth living and how individuals can thrive and flourish.

The value of Happiness :

As well quoted by Winston Churchill, 'The optimist sees opportunity in every difficulty. The pessimist sees difficulty in every opportunity.' This is Positive Psychology, which can help you become a champion in all times.

A son once asked his father, "Father, what is the value of happiness"? Father walked a mile and said "If you really want to understand the value of your life, theny you have to do as i say"Son agree. "Son, take this stone to market at roadside and then sit somewhere," the father remarked, passing him the stone he had purchased. Simply raise your two fingers if someone asks for the price. Don't forget to take it back home. When Sone saw that stone, she wondered why anyone would purchase such a basic item. Nevertheless, he followed his father's instructions and went to the market place. After sitting there for a while, an elderly woman approached him and said, "What is the worth of this stone?

The boy did not reply; he simply raised his two fingers in response to his father.When the woman saw that, she responded, "Okay, I'm ready to buy this stone for Rs. 200." The boy did as his father had told him and returned with the stone. Happily informed his father that a woman was willing to purchase it for Rs. 200."This time, you go to a museum," remarked the father.

Additionally, if someone asks you how much this stone is worth, please raise two fingers beforehand.Boy brought stone to museum. When that person viewed the stone, they inquired as to how much it cost. The boy simply held up two fingers without saying anything more.Boy brought stone to museum. When that person viewed the stone, they inquired as to how much it cost. The boy simply raised two fingers and didn't say anything else.Man answered, "Okay, twenty thousand.I'll buy it. The boy was shocked to learn that this music was worth this much. He returned home after declining to sell the stone once more. told everything to his father.

Then your dad stated, "Now ou take this stone to a precious stone shop and there too if someone ask you its price just raise two fingers" When the boy entered the stone business, the stone shopkeeper asked him right away, "How do you have this stone? Such a rarity. Buy this stone, please. Tell me the price you plan to sell it for. Silently, Biy lifted both of his fingers. The man said with joy, "Yes, I will buy it for two lakhs." Boys was taken aback once more. Once more, he returned home without selling the stone.

"Father, someone is ready to give 2 lakhs for this stone, sone for Rs. 200 only, while other was ready to give 20 thousand," he told his father after arriving home. Why is the difference so great?Dad clarified "You asked me to tell you the worth of your life, Son. These are your responses.With the aid of positive psychology, you may determine the worth of your life and then set this stone in place. Similar to how this stone's price varied depending on where you bought it. The same is true with lies. "The value of Positiveness of the way you live depends in where you place yourself"

The PERMA+ Model

The PERMA + model, developed by psychologist Martin Seligman, highlights five key elements essential for well-being:

P: Positive Emotion
E: Engagement
R: Relationships
M: Meaning
A: Accomplishment

Positive Emotion: This element emphasizes experiencing positive emotions such as joy, gratitude, and contentment. It involves cultivating a positive outlook on life and finding happiness in everyday experiences. *For example*, a person who finds joy in spending time with loved ones, appreciating nature, or pursuing hobbies is likely to have a higher level of well-being.

Engagement: Engagement refers to being fully absorbed and immersed in activities that are meaningful and enjoyable. It involves utilizing one's strengths to achieve a state of flow, where time seems to pass effortlessly because the individual is so engrossed in the task at hand. *An example* of engagement could be a musician who loses track of time while playing their instrument, or a writer who becomes completely absorbed in the process of writing a story.

Relationships: Building and maintaining meaningful relationships with others is crucial for well-being. Strong social connections provide support, companionship, and a sense of belonging, which contribute to overall happiness and fulfillment. *Examples* of nurturing relationships include close friendships, supportive family dynamics, and positive interactions with colleagues or peers.

Meaning-Finding meaning and purpose in life involves identifying values, goals, and activities that align with one's beliefs and aspirations. It's about feeling connected to something larger than oneself and understanding how one's actions contribute to the greater good. *For instance*, someone who volunteers at a local shelter may find a deep sense of meaning in helping those in need and making a positive impact on their community.

Accomplishment- Accomplishment entails setting and achieving goals, whether big or small, and experiencing a sense of competence and mastery. It involves recognizing one's abilities and accomplishments, as well as persevering through challenges and setbacks. *An example* of accomplishment could be completing a challenging project at work, finishing a marathon, or mastering a new skill like playing a musical instrument.

Each element of the PERMA model contributes to overall well-being, and individuals can enhance their quality of life by focusing on cultivating each aspect in their daily lives.

The "+" in PERMA

Optimism-Optimism means thinking positively and believing that good things will happen. For example, if you have an optimistic outlook, you might believe that even if things are tough now, they will get better in the future. People who are optimistic tend to be better at dealing with stress and are happier overall.

Physical Activity- Being physically active, like playing sports, going for a walk, or dancing, is really good for both your body and your mind. It helps you feel better emotionally, reduces feelings of sadness or anxiety, and helps you focus better. So, when you exercise, you not only get stronger physically but also feel happier and more clear-headed.

Nutrition-Eating healthy food is super important for both your body and mind. When you eat lots of fruits, vegetables, nuts, and seeds, you're giving your body the nutrients it needs to stay healthy. And guess what? It also helps your mood! Research shows that people who eat a balanced diet feel happier and have better mental health.

Sleep-Getting enough good-quality sleep is crucial for feeling good mentally and emotionally. When you sleep well, your brain gets a chance to rest and recharge, which helps you think more clearly and feel less stressed. On the other hand, if you don't sleep enough, it can make you feel moody, sad, or anxious.So, by being optimistic, staying active, eating healthy, and getting enough sleep, you can boost your overall wellbeing and feel happier and more resilient in life.

Chapter-2
Happiness

"Happiness is not something ready-made. It comes from your actions." - Dalai Lama

People search for happiness, however different people may have different definitions of it. Happiness is usually defined as an emotional state that is marked by joy, fulfilment, contentment, and satisfaction. Happiness can mean many various things, but it's commonly understood to involve pleasant emotions and a Life satisfaction.

A man asked the Buddha " I want happiness" Budda said first remove "I", that's Ego, then remove "want" , that's desure . See now you are left with only "Happiness".

The key of Happiness

Once upon a time in a small village, there lived a wise old man named Anand, which means "happiness" in his native language. Anand was known throughout the village for his constant and radiant happiness. People often wondered how he could be so content despite the challenges life brought.

One day, a curious young villager named Raj approached Anand and asked, "Old man, you always seem so happy. What is the secret to your happiness?"Anand smiled and said, "Come with me, and I will show you." He led Raj to a nearby river. There, he handed Raj a small, empty basket and instructed him, "Fill this basket with water from the river.

Raj was puzzled but did as he was told. He dipped the basket into the river, but as he lifted it, the water leaked out, leaving the basket empty. He tried again and again, but it was a futile task. He couldn't fill the basket with water.Frustrated and tired, Raj turned to Anand and said, "I can't do it. It's impossible to fill this basket with water."

Anand smiled and said, "Now, let me show you something." He handed Raj a solid, clay pot and asked him to fill it with water. Raj easily filled the pot without any water leakage.Anand explained, "Happiness is like this pot. It can hold your joy and contentment, just as the pot holds the water. The key to happiness is not in seeking to fill an empty basket but in having a heart that is like the clay pot, capable of holding and appreciating the simple joys of life."

Raj realized that he had been seeking happiness in external achievements and possessions, always wanting more, like the leaky basket. He learned that true happiness comes from within, from having a heart that is content with the present moment and grateful for life's blessings.From that day on, Raj changed his perspective and began to find happiness in the everyday moments of life, in the laughter of children, the warmth of the sun, and the beauty of the world around him. He learned the valuable lesson that the key to happiness lies not in what you have or what you achieve, but in how you perceive and appreciate the world with a heart like a clay pot—open, content, and full of joy.

Two key components of happiness are:

1.Emotional Balance
2.Life Balance

Emotional Balance:

Emotional balance refers to the ability to manage and regulate one's emotions effectively. It involves being able to experience a wide range of emotions, both positive and negative, without being overwhelmed by them. Emotional balance allows individuals to respond to life's challenges with resilience and adaptability, rather than being consumed by stress, anxiety, or depression. It involves practices such as mindfulness, self-awareness, and healthy coping mechanisms to maintain stability and well-being in the face of emotional ups and downs.

Life Balance:

Life balance, on the other hand, pertains to achieving harmony and equilibrium across various domains of life, such as work, relationships, leisure, and personal development. It involves prioritizing different aspects of life in a way that fosters fulfillment and satisfaction. Life balance means allocating time and energy to activities that align with one's values, goals, and priorities, while also ensuring that no single area dominates at the expense of others. This balance helps prevent burnout, fosters holistic well-being, and allows individuals to lead fulfilling and meaningful lives.Both emotional balance and life balance are interconnected and contribute significantly to overall happiness and well-being.

Dr. Y. Narasimha Raja

How to become happy person ?
Signs of Happiness

A boy lived there with an extremely wealthy family. In an attempt to demonstrate his kid how the impoverished live, his father took him on a trip into the country one day. So, he thought, they arrived to a very impoverished family's property. There, they stayed for several days. The father inquired about his son's enjoyment of the trip after they got back.

"Well, dad, it was awesome," the boy answered. Did you observe the lifestyles of the impoverished? The youngster answered, "Yes, I did." The father requested further information from his kid regarding his thoughts on their journey.Basically, they have four dogs, whereas we only have one. While their river never ends, our yard contains a swimming pool. Their heads are covered in stars at night, but our lanterns are very pricey. The entire horizon is theirs, and ours is the patio. Their fields are boundless, whereas ours is only a small plot of ground. Although they grow the food, we buy it. Their buddies keep them safe, so they don't need our high fence to safeguard our land.Father was quite surprised. There was nothing he could say.

"I appreciate you letting me see how poor we are," the youngster continued.The story demonstrates that financial possessions cannot determine one's genuine riches or level of happiness. What matters more than all is love, friendship, and freedom.

Happiness is a complex and subjective emotional state, but there are several common signs and indicators that may suggest someone is experiencing happiness. Keep in mind that these signs can vary from person to person, and the presence of one or more of these signs doesn't necessarily guarantee happiness. Here are some typical signs of happiness:

1. Positive mood
2. Smiling and Laughter
3. Don't compare with others
4. Bounceback
5. Peace of mind
6. Self appreciation
7. Sociability
8. Satisfaction
9. Relaxation
10. Optimisam

Positive Mood: A generally positive and upbeat mood characterized by optimism, enthusiasm, and a sense of joy. *An example for the Positive mood is morning school bell might not give good mood to the student, but definitely the evening school bell makes good mood. The bell is same and the bell timings are different. Happiness also depends on moods.*

Smiling and Laughter: One of the most obvious signs of happiness is a genuine and frequent smile, as well as spontaneous laughter. A smile serves as a warm greeting for all, symbolizing openness to all. Viewing the world with a smile makes everything appear more optimistic.

*Example of happy smile is **Chris Gayle**, the renowned cricketer hailing from Jamaica, represents the West Indies cricket team at the international level. His early life was marred by poverty, with his parents unable to afford his school fees. Gayle recounts resorting to collecting* *garbage and empty bottles from the streets to make ends meet, and even resorting to theft to satisfy his hunger.*

The left-handed batsman openly acknowledges that without cricket, he might have continued to lead a life of destitution. Despite facing numerous challenges and enduring insults, Gayle maintains a resilient demeanor, often wearing a smile on his face. His ability to remain cheerful in the face of adversity serves as an inspiring example, highlighting the remarkable power of a positive attitude.

1. **Don't compare with others**

"Comparison with myself brings improvement, comparison with others brings discontent." - Betty Jamie Chung

Comparing ourselves to others can rob us of happiness and creativity. It breeds feelings of inferiority and discontent, hindering our personal growth. Instead, we should focus on our own journey and strive to be better versions of ourselves. Comparing ourselves to others only leads to self-inflicted harm. Each of us has our own unique path in life, just like the sun and the moon - they shine in their own time and way.

*The best example is **Michael Phelps**, a 5-time Olympian, stands as a beacon of success in swimming, boasting an astounding 27 Olympic medals, 22 of which are gold, and setting 39 career world records. His achievements speak volumes, but Phelps's impact transcends mere statistics.*

He embodies qualities like inspiration, hope, and motivation, reminding us that anything is possible with dedication and perseverance. Phelps emphasizes the importance of extraordinary effort, highlighting that talent and past accomplishments are only stepping stones towards greatness.

Moreover, he advocates for setting goals that extend beyond personal ambition and encourages embracing failure as a catalyst for growth rather than allowing it to deter progress. Phelps underscores the significance of surrounding oneself with supportive individuals who believe in one's potential, reinforcing the notion that success is not achieved alone but through collective encouragement and collaboration.

2. Bounceback

"The true measure of success is how many times you can bounce back from failure." - Stephen Richards

Success isn't about never failing; it's about getting back up when you do fail. It's not how hard you fall, but how high you bounce back up that really matters. When you face setbacks and failures, it's just a part of the journey to reaching your goals. The most important thing in life isn't avoiding mistakes altogether, but learning from them and getting back on your feet each time you stumble.

Life isn't about how fast or how far you go, but how well you can recover from challenges. Turning setbacks into comebacks is like an art, and every failure is just another chance to start again, but smarter. Success isn't about never falling down; it's about how many times you can rise back up. And remember, it's not the challenges themselves that define us, but how we handle them and keep moving forward.

Example Worldclass allrounder cricketer **Mr.Yuvraj Singh** *in his linkdin has posted as flows about bounceback of sportsmanship.*

"Today, I want to share an important lesson I learned throughout my cricketing journey: the power of a victorious mindset.Rewind to 2007, the inaugural T20 World Cup. The moment when I hit six sixes in an over wasn't just about technique; it was a triumph of mindset. Facing a challenging bowler, I could have given into pressure. But I chose to believe in victory, in my ability to turn the game when we needed it.This mindset wasn't built overnight. It took years of practice, failures, and getting back up when life threw punches. Through my career, every time I walked onto the field, I carried not just the hopes of a nation but also a belief in myself. A belief that no matter the odds, victory was possible.This state of mind applies beyond cricket. In life, be it in your career or personal goals, the mindset of victory is crucial. It's about seeing challenges as opportunities to do better, and not as obstacles. It's about believing in your potential, even when others doubt you.

Throughout my career, especially during tough times like my battle with cancer, this mindset was my shield. It taught me that victory isn't just about winning matches, but instead, it's about overcoming your inner doubts and never giving up.So, to everyone facing challenges, just remember that your mindset can be your most powerful weapon. Cultivate it, nurture it, and let it guide you to your victories, both big and small.Stay strong and victorious!"

He was honored with the Player of the Tournament award for the ODI World Cup 2011. However, his performance saw a decline during the Test tour of England in the summer of the same year. Little did people know at that time that he was battling a cancerous tumor in his left lung.

Following this revelation, he underwent several months of chemotherapy at both the Cancer Research Institute in Boston and the Medical Facilities hospital in Indianapolis. He returned home in April, focusing on improving his physical fitness with the goal of returning to play for India.The resurgence of Yuvraj Singh in cricket could potentially be even more inspirational than his initial success.

3. Peace of mind

Peace of mind" refers to a state of inner calmness, tranquility, and contentment. It is a feeling of mental and emotional well-being, free from stress, anxiety, or worries. Achieving peace of mind often involves finding balance, acceptance, and inner harmony amidst life's challenges and uncertainties.

4. Self appreciation

Self-appreciation, in simple terms, means recognizing and valuing your own worth and qualities. It involves acknowledging your strengths, accomplishments, and positive attributes, as well as accepting and embracing your flaws and imperfections.Self-appreciation is about treating yourself with kindness and compassion. It means celebrating your achievements, no matter how small, and being proud of who you are.

Self-appreciation is like the starting point for getting better at things in your life. When you recognize your own value, it opens up lots of opportunities for you. When you appreciate yourself, you bring more positivity into your life. Self-appreciation is like the key that unlocks all your hidden talents and abilities.

Scientist Thomas Edision. Inventor of Light Bulb. Despite he faced numerous setbacks and failures along the way, Thomas remained determined to achieve his dream of inventing the light bulb.With each failed attempt, Thomas refused to be discouraged. Instead, he saw every setback as a valuable lesson, a step closer to success. When asked about his failures, Thomas responded with unwavering optimism, "I have not failed 10,000 times— I've successfully found 10,000 ways that will not work."

Finally, after years of perseverance and relentless effort, Thomas Edison successfully invented the light bulb, forever changing the course of history. His invention illuminated cities, homes, and hearts, bringing warmth and brightness to the darkest of nights. Through Thomas Edison's story, we learn the importance of self-appreciation and resilience.

5. **Sociability:** Being happy often involves spending time with friends and family, and enjoying social interactions.

6. **Satisfaction:** Feeling content and fulfilled with one's life, accomplishments, and relationships can lead to happiness.

7. **Relaxation:** Taking time to unwind and relax can contribute to feelings of happiness and well-being.

8. **Optimism:** Having a positive outlook on life and believing in the possibility of good things happening can increase happiness.

Types of Happiness

Once upon a time in a quaint little village there lived a humble cobbler named Tobias. Tobias wasn't a wealthy man by any means, but he possessed a heart overflowing with kindness and a spirit as resilient as the oak trees that dotted the landscape.

Despite the hardships he faced, Tobias found joy in the simplest of things. He took pleasure in the laughter of children as they played in the village square, in the warmth of the sun on his face as he worked in his tiny shop, and in the melody of birdsong that greeted him each morning.One day, a weary traveler stumbled into Tobias' shop seeking refuge from the relentless rain outside. The traveler, a weary merchant named Alaric, had journeyed far and wide in search of riches, but instead found himself burdened by loneliness and despair.

As Tobias welcomed the stranger into his humble abode, he noticed the heaviness in Alaric's eyes and the weariness etched into his brow. Sensing the traveler's troubles, Tobias offered him a seat by the crackling fire and a warm cup of tea.As the rain continued to drum against the window panes, Tobias and Alaric shared stories long into the night. Alaric spoke of his endless pursuit of wealth and success, of the sacrifices he had made along the way, and of the emptiness that gnawed at his soul.

Tobias listened intently, offering words of comfort and wisdom born from a lifetime of simple pleasures. He spoke of the beauty of friendship, the joy of giving without expecting anything in return, and the true meaning of happiness that could not be found in material possessions.As time went by, Alaric began to see the world through new eyes, finding beauty in the smallest of gestures and joy in the most unexpected places. He realized that true happiness wasn't found in the pursuit of wealth or success, but in the simple moments shared with others and the kindness of a compassionate heart.And so, in the company of his newfound friend Tobias and the gentle souls of the village, Alaric discovered a happiness that surpassed all his wildest dreams—a happiness that could only be found in the embrace of love, friendship, and the beauty of a life well-lived."

The distinction between hedonia and eudaimonia.

Happiness can be conceptualised in a multitude of ways. Greek philosopher Aristotle's views as follows

Hedonia:

- ❖ Focuses on maximizing pleasure and minimizing pain.Involves seeking immediate gratification and satisfaction of desires.
- ❖ Emphasizes short-term happiness and enjoyment.
- ❖ Examples include indulging in delicious food, engaging in leisure activities, and pursuing material possessions.

Eudaimonia:

- ❖ Centers on pursuing meaning, fulfillment, and personal growth.Involves striving for long-term well-being and flourishing.
- ❖ Emphasizes living in alignment with one's values and purpose.
- ❖ Examples include pursuing meaningful relationships, engaging in self-reflection and personal development, and contributing to the greater good of society.

Impact of Happiness

Happiness has a significant impact on various aspects of an individual's life and on society as a whole. The effects of happiness are wide-ranging here are some of the key impacts of happiness:

1. Psychological wellbeing
2. Physical health
3. Social and Interpersonal relationship
4. Productivity and achievement
5. Quality of Life
6. Community and service
7. Altruism and Prosocial behavior
8. creativity and Innovation
9. Environmental stewardship

Psychological Well-Being: Improved Mental Health: Happier individuals tend to experience lower rates of depression, anxiety, and other mental health issues.Resilience: Happy people are often better equipped to cope with stress and adversity, as they tend to exhibit higher levels of resilience.

Physical Health: Studies suggest that happier people tend to live longer and have a lower risk of chronic diseases and premature death.Happiness is associated with a stronger immune system, making individuals more resistaovernt to illness.

Social and Interpersonal Relationships: Happier people tend to have more satisfying and harmonious relationships with family, friends, and romantic partners.Social Connection: They are more likely to engage in social activities and have a stronger sense of community.

Productivity and Achievement: Happier individuals are often more productive, creative, and engaged in their work, which can lead to career success. Happier students may perform better academically and have a greater motivation to learn.

Quality of Life Happiness is a significant predictor of life satisfaction and overall well-being.

Community and Society: Happier societies often exhibit greater social cohesion, trust, and cooperation among members. Lower Crime Rates: Happier communities tend to have lower crime rates and better overall safety.

Altruism and Prosocial Behavior: Happy people are more likely to engage in acts of kindness, charity, and altruism.Community Involvement: They are often more involved in community and volunteer activities.

Creativity and Innovation: Happiness can foster a more open and creative mindset, leadirng to innovative thinking and problem-solving.

Environmental Stewardship: Happy individuals may be more inclined to engage in environmentally responsible behaviors and contribute to sustainability efforts.

Challenges of Finding Happiness

"Once upon a time in a small village, there lived a young boy named Raj. He was fascinated by kites and loved flying them in the open fields. Every evening, he would join other children in friendly kite-flying competitions, trying to keep his kite in the sky longer than anyone else.

One sunny day, Raj's grandfather, an elderly and wise man, gave him a beautifully crafted kite. It was colorful, with intricate designs that sparkled in the sun. He also handed Raj a strong and durable thread for flying the kite.With his new kite and thread, Raj was confident that he would win the upcoming competition. As he stood in the field, he watched as kites of all shapes and sizes soared into the sky. The competition was fierce, and the kites danced in the wind, each trying to outmaneuver the others.

Raj's kite, with its striking appearance, attracted the attention of everyone on the field. As he flew it higher and higher, he couldn't help but feel a sense of pride and superiority. But in his excitement, he lost focus on the strength of the thread that held his kite.Suddenly, a gust of wind tugged at the kite, and the thread began to slip from Raj's grasp. Panicking, he desperately tried to hold on, but the thread continued to slip through his fingers. Within moments, his beautiful kite was swept away by the wind and disappeared into the horizon.

Raj was devastated. He had lost not only the competition but also his cherished kite. He sat down in the field, feeling defeated and heartbroken.Seeing his grandson's distress, Raj's grandfather approached him and said, "Raj, I gave you a strong thread to hold your kite, but you were too focused on the kite's beauty and not on the thread's strength. The thread is like our character and values, which hold us steady in life's challenges."Raj nodded, realizing the wisdom in his grandfather's words. He had been so focused on the external, the appearance of the kite, that he had neglected the internal, the strength of the thread.

From that day on, Raj learned an important lesson about the value of inner strength and character. He understood that a beautiful appearance might capture attention, but it's the strength of one's values and character that keeps them grounded and resilient in the face of life's challenges. Raj went on to become a wiser and more humble young man, knowing that true strength came from within, just like the thread that held his kite aloft in the open sky.

The Positive Psychology is the Thread for your life

Finding happiness can be a challenging and complex journey due to various factors. Here are some of the challenges one might encounter when seeking happiness:

Personal Growth-The pursuit of happiness often requires personal growth and self-improvement, which can be challenging and sometimes uncomfortable.

"The butterfly needed to emerge through a little opening that happened to open up in the cocoon one day. When the child happened to walk by, he paused to observe the butterfly attempting to emerge from its cocoon. The gap remained the same, it took a long time, and the butterfly was trying extremely hard. Apparently, the butterfly's power was about to evaporate.To assist the butterfly, the boy made the decision. He cut through the cocoon with a penknife. Despite its fragile and feeble body and scarcely functioning wings, the butterfly managed to escape right away.Thinking that the butterfly would immediately expand its wings and take flight, the kid kept observing it. But that did not come to pass.

For its entire existence, the butterfly was forced to carry its feeble body and closed wings. Because the boy was unaware that the butterfly needed to make an effort to squeeze through the tiny opening in the cocoon in order for the life-giving fluid to transfer from its body to its wings and allow it to fly, the butterfly was unable to take flight. In order to grow stronger and enable it to continue growing and developing, life compelled the butterfly to emerge from its shell.We wouldn't be able to survive if we were spared all challenges in life. We face problems in life to help us grow as individuals.

Subjectivity: Happiness is a highly subjective and individual experience. What makes one person happy may not work for someone else. Understanding and defining what happiness means to you can be a challenge.

Expectations: Unrealistic expectations about happiness, often influenced by societal or cultural norms, can lead to disappointment and frustration.

Adaptation: The "hedonic treadmill" is the tendency to return to a baseline level of happiness after both positive and negative life events. This means that even after achieving something that brings happiness, the effect may be temporary.

External Influences: External circumstances, such as financial struggles, health issues, or challenging life events, can impact happiness. These external factors are sometimes beyond our control.

Comparisons: Constantly comparing oneself to others, especially in the age of social media, can lead to feelings of inadequacy and reduced happiness.

Cultural and Societal Pressures: Societal expectations, such as the pursuit of material wealth or a certain lifestyle, can divert individuals from what truly makes them happy.

Negative Emotions: Experiencing negative emotions is a natural part of life, and it's essential to acknowledge and process them. Avoiding or suppressing these emotions can hinder happiness.

Fear of Failure: The fear of failing in the pursuit of happiness can prevent individuals from taking risks and trying new experiences that could lead to greater well-being.

Overthinking: Overthinking, rumination, and excessive self-analysis can lead to stress and anxiety, undermining happiness.

Lack of Self-Compassion: Being overly critical of oneself and lacking self-compassion can impede the journey toward happiness.

Perfectionism: Striving for perfection can create unrealistic standards and result in constant dissatisfaction.

Unhealthy Coping Mechanisms: Turning to unhealthy coping mechanisms, such as substance abuse or excessive consumption, in response to stress and negative emotions can hinder happiness
.Loneliness: A lack of social connection and meaningful relationships can significantly impact happiness.

Lack of Purpose: Not having a sense of purpose or meaning in life can lead to feelings of emptiness and unhappiness.
Cognitive Biases: Cognitive biases, such as the negativity bias (focusing more on negative experiences), can affect one's perception of happiness.

Lack of Self-Awareness- Understanding one's values, strengths, and desires is essential for finding happiness. Without self-awareness, it's challenging to make choices that align with your well-being.

Environmental Factors: Societal and environmental factors, such as political instability, discrimination, and economic inequality, can make it more challenging for some individuals to find happiness.

Despite these challenges, it's important to remember that happiness is a dynamic and evolving state.

Chapter-3
Don't Overthink

Overthinking is the biggest cause of our unhappiness. Keep yourself occupied. Keep your mind off things that don't help you. Be optimistic." - Roy T. Bennett

Overthinking is when you spend too much time dwelling on something, like a problem or a decision, and you keep going over it in your mind again and again. It's like getting stuck on a thought loop, where you can't stop thinking about the same thing, even when it's not helpful or necessary. Overthinking can make you feel stressed, anxious, and confused, and it can make it hard to focus on other things or make decisions.

Have you ever watched a stone being thrown into a pond, Yes, and what happens? The stone disturbs the water and creates ripples. After some time, the ripples fade away and the pond returns to its calm state, that is like the mind. The stone is Overthinking. A single thought is like a stone thrown into the pond. If you throw stones continuously, the ripples will never settle. But if you allow them to, they eventually calm down. Similarly, if you keep indulging every thought, your mind will never find peace. stop overthinking

Research findings about Overthinking

In the book Who Think Too Much: How To Break Free of Overthinking and Reclaim Your Life," (2003, Henry Holt and Company). Among the findings" it's mentioned that overthinking is a big problem for many young and middle-aged adults. Surprisingly, it's less common among older adults

> - Overthinking is a big problem for young and middle-aged adults in the country. About 73% of 25-35 year-olds think too much, while only 52% of 45-55 year-olds and 20% of 65-75 year-olds do.
> - Overthinking can lead to serious depression and anxiety, especially in women. It also makes it hard to solve problems.
> - Women are more likely than men to overthink and get stuck because of it. About 57% of women and 43% of men overthink.
> - Overthinkers are more likely to use drugs or alcohol, and some might even think about or try to hurt themselves.

Overthinking can really mess with your happiness and mood. It's like making things worse in your head than they actually are. It's like creating problems that aren't even real. Overthinking makes us really unhappy. To feel better, try to stay busy and focus on things that make you feel good. Stay positive and don't worry too much about what could go wrong. Instead, think about what could go right!. Imagine overthinking is like sitting on a rocking chair. You're moving, but you're not going anywhere.

Sometimes, you just gotta let things happen instead of trying to control everything. Trust that things will work out okay. It's important to think things through, but don't let it stop you from taking action. And remember, thinking too much can put a strain on friendships and relationships because it makes us distant. So, it's okay to let go a little and just go with the flow of life.

Causes of Overthinking

1. You have more free time don't have any work . Stay busy for productive time.

None can destroy iron, but its own rust can. Likewise, none can destroy a person but his own mindset- Ratan Tata.

This quote by Ratan Tata, "None can destroy iron but its own rust," teaches us about the power of mindset and human resolve. Like iron can be corroded by rust, our mindset can lead us astray if we're not careful. It reminds us to be mindful of the thoughts we allow to influence us.

We are the gatekeepers of our minds, choosing which thoughts to let in. These thoughts shape our approach to challenges and life. Ratan Tata's quote inspires us to pay attention to our minds, where everything begins.Our personality, like iron, is strong and resilient. However, external influences like challenges and opportunities shape us. We must guard our character to filter these influences. If we let negative experiences define us, the outcome will reflect that.

Ultimately, we're in control of our lives, dreams, and passions. No one else can decide for us or determine our success or failure. Just like iron can only be affected by its rust, our personality is shaped by our own choices. Others can only motivate or influence us.

When you find yourself with free time and no work, it is devils mind, you start doing FOLLOWUPS, Whatsapp chats "How are you," eager to know others information and giving REMINDERS, Micromanagement, it's important to stay productive. Use this opportunity to engage in activities that enrich your life and contribute positively to your well-being. Whether it's pursuing hobbies, learning something new, volunteering, or taking care of tasks you've been putting off, staying busy can help you make the most of your time. By staying productive, you not only avoid boredom but also cultivate a sense of accomplishment and fulfillment. So, instead of letting idle time go to waste, seize the moment and make it meaningful by staying active and productive.

2. Gossip a tool for Overthinking

"Gossip is just a tool to distract people who have nothing better to do from feeling jealous of those few of us still remaining with noble hearts." - Anna Godbersen

Gossip is when people talk about others, often sharing personal or private information, rumors, or speculation. It's usually done in a casual or informal manner, and the information may or may not be true. Gossip can spread quickly through social circles, and it often involves discussing someone's behavior, relationships, or actions. While gossip can sometimes be harmless, it can also be hurtful or damaging, leading to misunderstandings, conflicts, and hurt feelings. It's important to be mindful of the impact of gossip and to avoid spreading rumors or sharing information that could be harmful to others.

Gossip / roumours is main seed of overthinking . Below mentioned story will tell abovt the drawbacks of Gossip/ roumours

Once, an elderly man spread rumors about his neighbor being a thief. Shortly after, a theft occurred in their neighborhood. The neighbor was arrested based on the rumors. But during the court trial, it was proven that the neighbor was innocent and not involved in the theft. The real thieves were caught by the police. The innocent neighbor was released from prison.

Feeling wronged, the innocent neighbor sued the old man for defaming him. In court, the old man argued that his words were harmless. The judge then asked the old man to write down his rumors on paper, tear them up, and scatter them on his way home.

The next day, the judge asked the old man to gather all the torn pieces of paper. The old man couldn't find them all, explaining that the wind had scattered them everywhere. The judge used this to show that just like the torn pieces of paper, the rumors had spread and couldn't be taken back, harming the neighbor's reputation.

The moral of the story is to be careful with your words because once spoken, they cannot be easily undone, and they can cause lasting harm to others.

"Gossip is the Devil's radio." - George Harrison

3. Confused mindset: -

The most confused you will ever get is when you try to convince your heart and spirit of something your mind knows is a lie."— Shannon L. Alder

In the heart of a lush forest, where sunlight filtered through the canopy of emerald leaves, there lived a gentle deer named Orion. Orion was known throughout the forest for his graceful leaps and his endearing innocence. But there was something peculiar about Orion—he possessed a fragrant navel.

It was said that every night as Orion slept beneath the starlit sky, his navel exuded a sweet, intoxicating fragrance that perfumed the air around him. The other forest creatures marveled at this phenomenon, attributing it to some mystical enchantment bestowed upon the deer by the forest spirits.However, what the animals didn't realize was that the fragrance emanated from within Orion himself. Deep within his being lay a reservoir of untapped talent, waiting to be discovered. But like the dear with its fragrant navel, Orion remained unaware of the extraordinary gift he possessed.

As Orion roamed the forest, he couldn't shake off a sense of restlessness and confusion. Despite the admiration he received from his fellow creatures for his external beauty and charm, he felt an emptiness gnawing at his soul. He yearned for something more, something beyond the superficial praise and admiration.One moonlit night, as Orion lay beneath the stars, his mind abuzz with questions and uncertainty, he heard a soft voice whispering in the gentle breeze. It was the voice of the *wise old owl, Athena, who perched on a nearby branch, her luminous eyes gazing intently at the deer.*

"Orion," she said in her melodious voice, "within you lies a talent so extraordinary, so wondrous, that even you are unaware of its existence."Orion's ears perked up at the owl's words, his heart fluttering with anticipation. With newfound determination, Orion embarked on a journey of self-discovery, delving deep into the recesses of his soul. He explored his passions, his dreams.He realized that true talent resided not in the external accolades and admiration of others, but in the depths of one's own being.And so, with his newfound wisdom and inner strength, Orion embraced his true self, sharing his gifts with the world and inspiring others to look within themselves to discover their own hidden talents.

Moral of the story is just like the dear with its fragrant navel, each of us holds within us a unique and extraordinary gift, Confusemind makes waiting to be uncovered and shared with the world. Identify internal talent and develop avoiding confusion mindset.

Cause of confused mindset

1. **External Influences:** Constant exposure to conflicting information, opinions, and societal expectations can overwhelm the mind, leading to confusion.
2. **Lack of Clarity:** Unclear goals, values, or priorities can leave individuals feeling directionless and uncertain about their choices.
3. **Overthinking:**Ruminating excessively on past events or worrying about the future can clutter the mind, making it difficult to focus or make decisions.
4. **Emotional Turmoil:** Strong emotions such as fear, anxiety, or sadness can cloud judgment and create confusion about how to navigate situations effectively.
5. **Self-Doubt:** A lack of confidence in one's abilities or decisions can breed uncertainty and indecision, fueling a cycle of confusion.
6. **Information Overload:** In today's digital age, the abundance of information available can be overwhelming, leading to cognitive overload and mental fatigue.
7. **Lack of Self-Awareness:** Failing to understand one's own strengths, weaknesses, and values can result in inner conflict and confusion about personal identity and purpose.
8. **External Validation:** Seeking approval and validation from others instead of trusting one's own instincts can lead to confusion about one's true desires and priorities.

How to overcome from the confusemindset Mindfulness Practices:

Engage in mindfulness meditation, deep breathing exercises, or yoga to ground yourself in the present moment and quiet the noise of confusion in your mind.

Clarify Goals and Priorities:

Take time to reflect on your values, aspirations, and what truly matters to you. Clarifying your goals and priorities can provide a sense of direction and clarity amidst confusion.

Break Tasks into Manageable Steps:

When faced with overwhelming tasks or decisions, break them down into smaller, more manageable steps. Focus on one step at a time, reducing the complexity and easing the burden of confusion.

Seek Clarity Through Communication:

Reach out to trusted friends, family members, or mentors for guidance and support. Sometimes, discussing your thoughts and feelings with others can help bring clarity to your situation.

Practice Self-Compassion:

Be kind to yourself during times of confusion. Understand that confusion is a natural part of the human experience and treat yourself with the same compassion and understanding you would offer to a friend in need.

Embrace Uncertainty:

Accept that uncertainty is a normal aspect of life and an opportunity for growth. Instead of resisting uncertainty, embrace it as a chance to learn, explore, and discover new possibilities.

Take Breaks and Rest:

Allow yourself time to rest and recharge when feeling overwhelmed by confusion. Engage in activities that bring you joy and relaxation, allowing your mind to reset and regain clarity.

Challenge Negative Thoughts:

Identify and challenge any negative or self-limiting beliefs that contribute to your confusion. Replace them with more positive and empowering thoughts that support your well-being and growth.

Focus on Solutions:

Instead of dwelling on the source of confusion, focus your energy on finding solutions and taking action. Break down the problem into manageable parts and brainstorm potential solutions to move forward.

Seek Professional Help if Needed:

If confusion persists and significantly impacts your daily life, consider seeking support from a therapist or counselor. Professional guidance can provide valuable insights and strategies for overcoming confusion and building mental resilience.

Other factors influencing Overthinking :-

- ✓ Lack of Motivation
- ✓ Lack of Tust
- ✓ Low self-esteem (self doubt, confidence)
- ✓ Over emotions
- ✓ Strained relationship
- ✓ Ego (considering themselves superiors)
- ✓ Mental health
- ✓ Over Reaction
- ✓ Over Protection
- ✓ Over involvement in others matter.
- ✓ Habits
- ✓ Over planning and less execution.
- ✓ Creating Conflicts
- ✓ Over perfection
- ✓ Micro level comparison

Chapter-4

Emotional Intelligence

"Emotional intelligence is the key to both personal and professional success." — Daniel Goleman

Until now, we have acknowledged the significant role played by Intelligence Quotient (IQ) in life, but it is merely one aspect. Another equally crucial dimension exists, known as Emotional Intelligence or Emotional Quotient (EQ), which contributes to fostering a positive mindset.Emotional intelligence, also known as EI or EQ (emotional quotient), encompasses the capacity to perceive, interpret, manage, and utilize emotions effectively in communication and relationships.

Emotional intelligence is not about being soft. It's about being smart with your emotions

Emotional Intelligence offers a pathway to transform potentially negative emotional reactions into positive, constructive responses. It starts with cultivating self-awareness, recognizing and understanding our own emotions—a fundamental skill essential for navigating both personal and professional environments.

This skill involves not only expressing and regulating one's emotions but also understanding, interpreting, and responding to the emotions of others. Many experts argue that emotional intelligence holds greater significance than IQ in achieving success and fulfillment in life, emphasizing its pivotal role in navigating social interactions, resolving conflicts, and fostering constructive relationships.

Inour life the contribution of IQ is only 20% and remaiing 80% is from the emotional intelligence. This might include self motivation, perseistence, impulsive control, mood regularisation, empathy and other factors.Remember IQ and EQ are not enemies. Both are executing work together. The jointwork of IQ and EQ will lead for the decision making.

Low EQ leads sucides :-

A person with high IQ mght be brilliant, but if he don't have control over his Emotions, he himself will be problem for his life. Till now we belive that the IQ people those are topper in the examinations, by position in the corporate are successful. But IQ can not bring the happiness and life satisfaction in the life. We have witnessed the great scietists, multi billionaire, actors, doctors, politicians have more IQ and they might have low EQ they have committed sucides.

They have not judge the Emotions and situations properly.

Nobel prize winner four scientist committed sucides They included four Nobel Prize winners: Emil

Fischer (1852-1919), Hans Fischer (1881-1945), Percy Bridgman (1882-1961), and Stanford Moore (1913 - 1982), as well as others of similar caliber, like the Austrian physicist Ludwig Boltzmann (1844-1906).
The highest IQ multi billionaires committed sucide Low EQ

In our society, the pursuit of wealth is often intertwined with dreams and aspirations, with the belief that money can bring happiness and success. However, this narrative overlooks the complexities of human experience. The pressure to succeed can be overwhelming, leading to mental strain that manifests in various forms of stress, irrespective of circumstances. Tragically, even individuals with substantial financial resources are not immune to the challenges of mental health. Here are examples of successful businessmen who tragically took their own lives:

➤ Jonathan Wraith, a young British millionaire, unexpectedly ended his life, possibly overwhelmed by familial concerns.
➤ Eli M. Black, a Jewish-American businessman, faced ruin due to scandal, ending his life by jumping from his office building.
➤ Huibert Boumeester, a Dutch millionaire banker, succumbed to depression following a major corporate takeover, leaving behind a note expressing his despair.
➤ Christopher Foster, despite being a wealthy businessman, took his own life after financial troubles pushed him to a breaking point.

- John Lawrenson and his wife ended their lives together as she battled cancer, unable to face the prospect of life without her.
- Wayne Pai, a respected Taiwanese businessman, died amidst allegations of impropriety, leaving behind a cloud of suspicion.
- Paul Castle, a prominent figure in British society, took his own life amidst financial setbacks and personal struggles.
- Peter Smedley, a successful hotelier, chose to end his life due to severe illness, a decision documented by the BBC.
- Howard Worthington's life ended tragically after a violent incident, highlighting the destructive consequences of unchecked emotions.
- ReiJane Huai, a former CEO, ended his life following legal troubles, leaving behind a legacy of innovation overshadowed by tragedy.

These heartbreaking stories offer no immunity to the struggles of the human condition, underscoring the importance of mental health awareness and support.

The Highest IQ = EQ will contribute to lead the happy, relationship, social life successful life.

Cristiano Ronaldo grew up as the youngest of four siblings in a household filled with pride but also struggles. His mother, Dolores Aveiro, worked tirelessly as a cook and cleaner to make ends meet. The family's financial hardship was so severe that Dolores once considered terminating her pregnancy, resorting to a homemade remedy, as revealed in her book "Mother Courage." Despite the challenges, Cristiano emerged with a strong-willed spirit, as he humorously remarked to his mother, "Look mum, you wanted to abort me, and now I'm the one who's pulling the purse-strings in the house."

Additionally, his personal life has been marked by moments of drama and trauma, adding layers of complexity to his already remarkable story.Ronaldo experienced bullying from teammates and rivals while he was a player for the club. He effortlessly overcome all of these problems because he is a powerful person on the inside as well as out. Some people refer to him as a crybaby. Nonetheless, he aspires to be the best in whatever he does, and disappointment brings him to tears. Anything wrong with that?

The news of the fourth was finally shared with Ronaldo's family. The family realised they would never be able to pay the bills, even with his father's job.Due to their still-tight financial situation, he and his buddies had to go to the nearby McDonald's and request leftover meals.When Ronaldo was fourteen years old, he took the momentous decision to quit school and dedicate his life to football. Academic pursuits didn't interest him, as he envisioned a future as a village fisherman. However, his true passion lay in football, prompting him to leave school at the age of 14 to devote himself entirely to the sport.

He was given a year later a diagnosis of racing heart syndrome, which required cardiac surgery to treat. According to medical professionals, quitting football permanently was the only alternative choice.But the child, a WARRIOR, decided on surgery. Following a successful operation, Ronaldo resumed his activities. With the goal of becoming the greatest football player of all time, Ronaldo began training day and night.

Ronaldo was practising by himself while everyone else went to take a shower. To get better at dribbling and balancing, he even went into the wilderness to practise. Cristiano Ronaldo's journey in football is a testament to his unparalleled excellence. From his professional debut with Sporting Lisbon in 2003 to his return to Manchester United in 2021 as the all-time leading scorer in international men's football, Ronaldo has consistently achieved greatness. He won numerous titles, including FA Cup and UEFA Champions League trophies with Manchester United, and Serie A with Juventus. His leadership led Portugal to victory in the UEFA European Championship in 2016. Alongside his club successes, Ronaldo earned multiple FIFA Ballon d'Or awards, highlighting his individual brilliance. These milestones illustrate Ronaldo's enduring impact on the sport and cement his legacy as one of football's greatest players.

Different Theories of Emotions

There are several theories on emotions and emotional intelligence; here, Robert Plutchik's and Daniel Goleman's theories have been taken for better understanding

Robert Plutchik's Wheel of Emotions

It is a model that categorizes human emotions into primary and secondary emotions, arranged in a wheel-like diagram. Robert Plutchik's theory of emotions identifies eight primary or basic emotions, each with its opposite, resulting in a total of sixteen emotions. The eight primary emotions are:

1. *Joy:* A feeling of happiness, contentment, or delight.
2. *Sadness:* A state of unhappiness, sorrow, or grief.
3. *Anger:* A strong feeling of displeasure, hostility, or irritation.
4. *Fear:* An emotion triggered by perceived threats or danger.
5. *Trust:* A sense of confidence, reliance, or belief in someone or something.
6. *Disgust:* A strong aversion or revulsion towards something unpleasant or offensive.
7. *Surprise:* A sudden, unexpected reaction to something unforeseen or unusual.
8. *Anticipation:* An eager expectation or excitement about future events or outcomes.

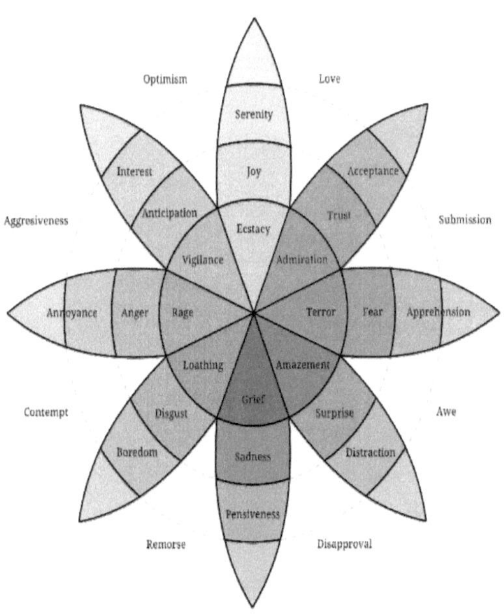

Each of these primary emotions can combine with one another to form more complex emotional states, resulting in a wide range of feelings and experiences.

Daniel Goleman and Richard E Boyatzis.

Harward Business Review has published an articleon 6th Feb 2017 Emotional Intelligence has 12 elements. Which do you need to work on ? by Daniel Goleman and Richard E Boyatzis.

Daniel Goleman is a well-known Author, psychologist, and expert in emotional intelligence. He helped bring the concept of emotional intelligence into the spotlight, which was first introduced by Peter Salovey and John Mayer in 1990. Goleman developed a framework consisting of five main components that make up emotional intelligence. He also emphasized that these skills can be learned and improved by anyone.

The primary emotions

A joy, trust, fear, surprise, sadness, disgust, anger, and anticipation. Each primary emotion is paired with its opposite on the wheel. For example, joy opposes sadness, trust opposes disgust, fear opposes anger, and surprise opposes anticipation.

The secondary emotions

There are blends of the primary emotions, resulting in more nuanced emotional states. For instance, anticipation plus joy creates optimism, while anticipation plus fear results in anxiety. The Wheel of Emotions provides a visual representation of the complex interplay between different emotional states and their relationships. It helps individuals understand and articulate their feelings, facilitating emotional awareness and regulation

Emotional Intellegence Domains

1. Self-awareness
2. Self-management
3. Social awareness
4. Relationship management

Emotional Intelligence Domains and Competencies

Self-awareness	Self-management	Social awareness	Relationship management
Emotional self-awareness	Emotional self-control	Empathy	Influence
	Adaptability		Coach and mentor
	Achievement orientation	Organizational awareness	Conflict management
	Positive outlook		Teamwork
			Inspirational leadership

1. Self-awareness :-

Knowing and understanding your own Strenths, Areas of Improvments (Limitations) & feelings. It's also about understanding how your actions and moods affect other people. When you're self-aware, you know what you're good at and what you're not so good at. Goleman says that people who are self-aware usually have a good sense of humor, feel confident about themselves, and understand how others see them.

Qualities :-

- ✓ Knows own Strenghts, Weakness, Opportunities, Threats.
- ✓ Self Confident
- ✓ Knows self limitations- few works they can perform , some not. They find the way to overcome.
- ✓ Goals
- ✓ Self and others values

(The self awareness is the first Competence, this topic has mentioned in the Emotional Compentence)

2. Self Management :-

Managing your emotions and managing your feelings. Emotional self-control, adaptability, achievement orientation, and a positive outlook fall under self-management.

In a city, a prestigious institution offered coaching to unemployed youth, aiming to secure jobs in banks. With a maximum intake of 50 students per batch, competition was fierce. Mr. A and Mr. B both aspired to enrol but were delayed by two days. By then, all slots were filled.

In frustration, Mr. A vented anger at the teachers, abused, hurling insults for denying him admission. Conversely, Mr. B approached with grace, expressing his eagerness and understanding the situation.

I am very much interested in joining your institution. As admissions are currently closed, I may not be able to secure a spot. However, I kindly request that if any students drop out from the course in the future, you consider offering me the opportunity to join.

The next day, a slot vacant due to a dropout. The institution faced a dilemma: offer the spot to Mr. A, who had abused and insulted, or to Mr. B, who had shown humility.

In the end, the majority leaned towards Mr. B. This decision illustrated the importance of self-management in interactions with others. Mr. B's respectful demeanour proved more favourable, emphasizing the significance of handling situations with grace and composure. Here the situation is same for both Mr.A & Mr. B. It depends how we handle the emotional situation. If Mr. A could understand the situation and act accordingly, then Mr. A also get probability to get the admission. The conclusion is Mr. A's EQ was very poor and where as Mr.B'sEQ was very high.

Self Management EI Domains

1. Emotional self-control
2. Adaptability
3. Achievement orientation
4. Positive outlook

❖ Emotional Self-Control

Self-control is the ability to keep disruptive emotions and impulses in check. ***Example:***Imagine you're in a heated meeting where a colleague criticizes your work. Instead of reacting angrily or defensively, you take a deep breath, listen calmly, and respond thoughtfully, addressing their concerns without losing your temper.

❖ Adaptability

Adaptability involves being flexible and adjusting to new circumstances or changes in the environment. ***Example:***You are leading a project, and midway through, there is a significant change in the client's requirements. Instead of becoming frustrated or anxious, you quickly adapt your plans and communicate the new direction clearly to your team, ensuring everyone remains focused and motivated.

❖ Achievement Orientation

Achievement orientation means striving to meet or exceed a standard of excellence. ***Example:*** You set a personal goal to improve your public speaking skills. Despite your busy schedule, you manage your time effectively to practice regularly, seek feedback, and attend workshops, gradually becoming a more confident and skilled speaker.

❖ **Positive Outlook: -**

A positive outlook involves maintaining an optimistic and hopeful perspective, even in challenging situations. It means focusing on the good, finding opportunities in difficulties, and believing in positive outcomes. For example, consider a person who loses their job. Instead of dwelling on the loss, they view it as an opportunity to pursue a more fulfilling career, learn new skills, or start their own business. This optimistic mindset not only boosts their resilience but also inspires those around them. By maintaining a positive outlook, individuals can navigate life's ups and downs more effectively and encourage others to do the same.(For more details refer Emotional Competencies)

3.Social Awarness:-

Mastering the fundamental people skills. Understand others feelings. These people are more popular, outgoing,more sensitive.   Social awareness have competencies of Empathy and Organizational awareness. These are emphasized in the competencies. Social awareness is having four categories

1. Antipathy
2. Apathy
3. Sympathy
4. Empathy

❖ **Antipathy (**Below 0% EQ and Negative EQ)

Antipathy refers to a strong feeling of dislike or hostility towards someone or something. It involves conflicting interests. It is distinct from simply disagreeing In interpersonal relationships, antipathy can create tension, conflict, and barriers to effective communication and collaboration.

For example, Mr. A failed the exam due to a shortage of one mark. He would like to express his emotions to Mr. B. Then Mr. B has reacted in a negative way, saying, 'You are not a good student, and it's good that you failed the examination.' This type of negative attitude refers to antipathy.

❖ **Apathy** (0% EQ i.e very Low EQ)

Apathy refers to a lack of interest, enthusiasm, or concern about important matters or activities. In the context of emotional intelligence, apathy can hinder individuals from connecting with others, understanding their own emotions, or engaging in meaningful relationships and pursuits.

Neutral emotions *For example, Mr. C has won the gold medal in the National Swimming competition. Mr. C wanted to share his achievement with Mr. D. However, Mr. D did not respond to this accomplishment. He said, 'We can discuss it after a week,' and ignored further communication, thereby straining the relationship. Mr. D either he is not responded positively or negatively. This kind of status quo of neutralisam is called A pathy. Apathi is zero emotions and better than Antipath negative emotions.*

❖ Sympathy

It differs from empathy in that empathy. Sympathy can Identify others problem, but can not able help others or solve problems. It is the ability to understand and share the feelings of another person. It involves feelings that can not able help others effectively. Sympathy is often expressed through supportive words, gestures of kindness, or acts of empathy.

For example, Mr. A failed the examination by just one mark. He would like to express his feelings to Mr. E. While Mr. E listens to Mr. A's feelings, he does not offer any assistance or support to solve the issue. There is no motivation provided to help Mr. A overcome the challenge.

❖ Empathy :-

Goleman defines empathy as the ability to understand and share the feelings of another person. It involves putting oneself in someone else's shoes and comprehending their emotions, thoughts, and perspectives. In empathy, we realize others' pains as our own. We accompany them to events such as movies and picnics, providing them with an opportunity to alleviate stress. Sharing time with them is a demonstration of high emotional intelligence (EQ).

Types of Empathy

1.Cognitive Empathy

2. Emotional Empathy

❖ Cognitive Empathy

Cognitive empathy is the ability to understand another person's perspective or mental state. Example:A manager notices that one of their team members is consistently submitting work late. Instead of reprimanding them immediately, the manager takes time to understand the underlying reasons. They talk to the employee and discover that they are facing personal challenges at home. By understanding the employee's situation, the manager can provide the necessary support and adjustments to help improve their performance.

❖ Emotional Empathy :

Emotional empathy is the capacity to share the feelings of another person and actually feel what they are experiencing on an emotional level.

Example:A friend is grieving the loss of a loved one. Instead of just saying, "I'm sorry for your loss," you genuinely feel their sorrow and provide comfort by spending time with them, listening to their feelings, and even crying with them. This shared emotional experience helps the grieving friend feel understood and less alone in their pain.

By practicing both cognitive and emotional empathy, we can enhance our ability to connect with others, support them effectively, and demonstrate high emotional intelligence.

4. Relationship Management

We cannot control destiny or time, nor can we hold onto heartbeats and life, but we can maintain good relationships, and that's something to cherish forever.

Relationship management involves nurturing and maintaining positive connections with others, whether personal or professional. It's about building trust, understanding, and effective communication to foster mutually beneficial relationships. In business, this includes strategies for maintaining strong connections with clients, customers, partners, and stakeholders through regular communication, excellent customer service, and prompt issue resolution. In personal relationships, it means being attentive, supportive, and empathetic, and investing time and effort into sustaining meaningful connections with friends, family, and loved ones.

Five Elements of Daniel Goleman's Emotional Intelligence Framework

1. **Influence:** The ability to persuade and positively impact others' thoughts, feelings, and actions.

2. **Coaching and Mentoring:** Guiding and developing others to reach their full potential through support, feedback, and encouragement.

3. **Conflict Management:** Handling disagreements constructively, finding solutions that satisfy all parties involved.

4. **Teamwork:** Collaborating effectively with others, fostering a sense of unity and cooperation within a group or team.

5. **Inspirational Leadership:** Motivating and energizing others by communicating a compelling vision and leading by example.

 (More details are furnished in the Emotional competencies)

Emotional competencies

1. Selfawareness
2. Emotional self-control
3. Adaptability
4. Achievement orientation
5. Positive outlook
6. Empathy
7. Organizational awareness
8. Influence
9. Coaching &mentoring
10. Conflict management
11. Teamwork
12. Inspirational leadership

1. **Self-awareness :-**

Knowing and understanding your own Strengths, Areas of Improvements (Limitations) & feelings. It's also about understanding how your actions and moods affect other people. When you're self-aware, you know what you're good at and what you're not so good at. Goleman says that people who are self-aware usually have a good sense of humor, feel confident about themselves, and understand how others see them.

Qualities, Knows own Strengths, Weakness, Opportunities, Threats.Self Confident. Knows self limitations- few works they can perform , some not. They find the way to overcome. They are goal oreiented. Respect self and others values.

2. *Emotional Self Control*

Emotional self-control is all about managing our emotions and impulses, especially when things get tough. It's about staying calm and composed, even when we feel overwhelmed or upset. Put simply, it means keeping it together no matter how intense our feelings.

When we have emotional self-control, we can:

- ➤ Stay focused and think clearly, even in stressful situations.
- ➤ Handle conflicts in a constructive and productive way.
- ➤ Create more positive interactions with others.
- ➤ Encourage others to give their best effort and ideas.

In essence, emotional self-control helps us navigate challenges effectively and maintain positive relationships with those around us.

Special Qualities :-

> *Handle "Complex situation in simple manner*
> *Proactive, They know what & how to ask and how to behave.*
> *They make others Important in the situation*
> *The give more respect to others, hence these people also get the respect from others.*

3. Adaptability

Emotional adaptability, as described by Daniel Goleman, refers to the ability to adjust and respond effectively to changing emotional situations and demands. It involves being flexible in how we perceive, understand, and manage our emotions in various circumstances. People with high emotional adaptability can quickly recover from setbacks, navigate through transitions, and thrive in unpredictable or challenging environments. They can maintain a sense of balance and composure, even when faced with unexpected emotional triggers. Emotional adaptability is an essential component of emotional intelligence, enabling individuals to navigate life's ups and downs with resilience and grace.

4. Achievement Orientation

Daniel Goleman's concept of Achievement Orientation is a key aspect of emotional intelligence (EI). It involves the drive to set and achieve challenging goals, as well as the ability to persist in the face of obstacles and setbacks. Goleman emphasizes that individuals with high achievement orientation are motivated by a desire for excellence rather than external rewards alone. They possess a strong sense of purpose, take initiative, and are proactive in pursuing their objectives. Additionally, they exhibit resilience and adaptability, learning from failures and using setbacks as opportunities for growth. Goleman's work underscores the importance of achievement orientation in personal and professional success, highlighting its role in driving innovation, productivity, and fulfillment.

5. Positive Outlook

"Positive Outlook" refers to the ability to maintain an optimistic and hopeful attitude, even in the face of challenges or adversity.

It is a key aspect of emotional intelligence and involves seeing the brighter side of situations, focusing on solutions rather than problems, and finding opportunities for growth and learning. Individuals with a positive outlook are resilient in the face of setbacks, able to bounce back from disappointments, and maintain a sense of optimism about the future. Goleman emphasizes that cultivating a positive outlook can lead to greater resilience, improved mental health, and enhanced overall well-being.

6. Empathy

Goleman defines empathy as the ability to understand and share the feelings of another person. It involves putting oneself in someone else's shoes and comprehending their emotions, thoughts, and perspectives. In empathy, we realize others' pains as our own. We accompany them to events such as movies and picnics, providing them with an opportunity to alleviate stress. Sharing time with them is a demonstration of high emotional intelligence (EQ).

Types of Empathy

1. Cognitive empathy
2. Emotional empathy.

Cognitive empathy

Cognitive Empathy is the ability to understand another person's perspective intellectually, Cognitive empathy involves intellectually understanding another person's perspective without necessarily sharing their emotions

For example, Mr. G is a friend of Mr. H. Mr. G has been hospitalized for a month due to an accident in the city. During this time, his family members are unable to arrange transportation to and from the hospital, as well as to pick up and drop off their children from school and home. In this situation, Mr. H empathizes with Mr. G's family and offers his assistance. He does not ignore the needs of his friend during this difficult time. This act of kindness falls under the category of empathy.

➢ **Listening and Understanding:** When someone shares their point of view or experiences, you actively listen and comprehend their thoughts and reasoning without necessarily feeling the same emotions they are expressing.

> **Putting Yourself in Their Shoes:** You can imagine how someone might feel or think in a particular situation based on their background, personality, or past experiences, even if you don't feel the same way yourself.

> **Recognizing Different Perspectives:** You understand that people may have different opinions, beliefs, or values than your own, and you can appreciate their viewpoint even if you don't agree with it.

> **Problem-Solving from Another's Perspective:** In a professional setting, you can anticipate how a colleague or client might react to a decision or proposal based on their interests, priorities, and concerns, allowing you to tailor your approach accordingly.

> **Empathetic Listening:** You can engage in empathetic listening, where you focus on understanding the other person's perspective and validating their feelings without necessarily experiencing the same emotions yourself.

Emotional empathy

It involves feeling and sharing the emotions of others. Emotional empathy is about not just understanding another person's emotions but also experiencing those emotions alongside them. Here are some examples:

- ➤ **Feeling Sadness:** When a friend shares that they are feeling sad because of a recent loss, you also start to feel sadness and may even tear up in response to their emotions.
- ➤ **Sharing Joy:** If someone close to you achieves something significant and feels elated, you might find yourself sharing in their happiness and feeling genuinely joyful for their success.
- ➤ **Experiencing Anxiety:** When a family member expresses their worries and fears about an upcoming event, you start to feel anxious and may experience similar sensations of nervousness.
- ➤ **Empathetic Crying:** Witnessing someone else cry can trigger your own tears, even if you're not directly affected by the situation, simply because you're empathizing with their emotional pain.
- ➤ **Feeling Anger on behalf of others:** If a colleague shares a frustrating experience they had at work, you might feel a surge of anger on their behalf, understanding their perspective and feeling indignant about the unfair treatment they received.

In emotional empathy, there's a shared emotional experience where you connect with the other person's feelings on a deeper level, often mirroring or resonating with their emotions.

7. Organiztional awareness

Organizational awareness involves understanding an organization's structure, culture, and informal networks. It includes recognizing how the organization operates, identifying key players, and understanding power dynamics that influence decision-making. This awareness helps individuals navigate the organization, build strategic relationships, and align their actions with organizational goals.

The Orgznizational awareness have following components

- Understanding the Organizational Structure
- Recognizing Organizational Culture
- Navigating Informal Networks
- Awareness of Power Dynamics
- Awareness of Power Structures:
- Sensitivity to Organizational Politics
- Knowledge of Stakeholders
- Reading Organizational Signals
- Adaptability and Flexibility

8. Influence

Influence, as the ability to have a positive impact on others to gain their support, intersects with emotional intelligence (EI), which involves understanding and using emotions constructively.

Joseph Schooling's journey from a star-struck teenager to challenging his idol, Michael Phelps, for Olympic medals exemplifies the transformative power of dedication and determination in the pursuit of excellence.

In 2008, a young Schooling posed next to Phelps, his swimming idol, before the Beijing Olympics. Over the following eight years, Schooling's passion and talent propelled him to remarkable achievements in the pool, culminating in his historic performance at the Rio Olympics.On August 12, 2016, Schooling made history by becoming the first Singaporean man to reach an Olympic swimming final. With a time of 50.83 seconds in the 100m butterfly semi-final, he not only set a new national record but also outpaced a field that included Phelps, the most decorated Olympian of all time.

Despite once watching Phelps's races endlessly and counting every stroke, Schooling remained focused on charting his own path in the sport. He beat Phelps's age-group time in the 100 yards butterfly and aimed to surpass more of his records.

9. Coaching and Mentoring

Coaching and mentoring are both strategies centered around one-on-one dialogue aimed at improving an individual's skills, knowledge, or job performance. Despite their frequent interchangeability, there are distinctions between the two.Coaching coaches in the workplace are not the same as counselors, psychotherapists, gurus, instructors, trainers, or consultants. Professional coaching, often carried out by qualified practitioners, aims to enhance clients' effectiveness and performance, facilitating their realization of full potential.

Coaching involves an experienced individual, known as a coach, aiding a learner or client in attaining specific personal or professional goals through instruction and support. During a coaching session, typically conducted as a dialogue between the coach and the coachee, the focus lies on guiding the coachee to discover solutions independently

Example :- Indian cricket former coach Gary Kirsten. Kirsten's tenure as the coach of the Indian cricket team from 2008 to 2011 marked a significant chapter in cricket history. His leadership was instrumental in guiding the team to one of its most coveted victories: the 2011 Cricket World Cup. The pinnacle of Kirsten's coaching career with India was undoubtedly the triumph in the 2011 Cricket World Cup, a momentous occasion that brought joy to millions of fans across the country. This victory ended a decades-long wait for India, with their last World Cup win dating back to 1983. Kirsten's strategic insights, meticulous planning, and ability to nurture talent played a pivotal role in shaping the team into world-beaters.

Throughout his coaching career, Kirsten was known for his friendly demeanor and his ability to forge strong bonds with his team members. His approachability and genuine care for the players fostered a positive team environment, enabling them to perform at their best on the field. Kirsten's contribution to the Indian cricket team is remembered as integral to their respective journeys in the world of cricket.

Top 10 Coaching skills

1. Technical proficiency in the sport/activity.

2. Clear and effective communication.
3. Motivating and inspiring athletes.
4. Adaptability to individual needs and team dynamics.
5. Strong leadership on and off the field.
6. Emotional intelligence in handling athletes' emotions.
7. Providing constructive feedback and guidance.
8. Creating a positive and supportive team environment.
9. Strategic planning and tactical awareness.
10. Continuous learning and professional development.

Mentoring

Mentoring is a developmental relationship in which a more experienced or knowledgeable individual (the mentor) provides guidance, support, and advice to a less experienced or knowledgeable individual (the mentee). Mentoring typically involves a long-term relationship focused on the mentee's personal and professional growth, career development, and skill enhancement.

Mentors offer insights, share their experiences, provide constructive feedback, and help mentees navigate challenges and opportunities. The goal of mentoring is to empower mentees to reach their full potential, achieve their goals, and succeed in their endeavors.

The difference between Mentoring and Coaching

Aspect	Coaching	Mentoring
Purpose	Achieving specific goals or performance improvements	Overall career development and personal growth
Focus	Short-term, task-oriented	Long-term, holistic development
Relationship	Coach-client; may not have direct experience in the client's field	Mentor-mentee; mentor typically more experienced
Structure	Structured, time-bound sessions	Informal, ongoing relationship
Accountability	Emphasis on individual ownership and accountability	Less direct accountability, more guidance and advice
Expertise	Focuses on guiding the individual towards self-discovery and solutions	Provides advice, wisdom, and perspective based on experience
Duration	Typically shorter engagements	Longer-term relationships

10. Conflict Management

Conflict arises when individuals experience differences in their thought processes, attitudes, comprehension, interests, needs, and sometimes even perceptions. These differences can manifest in various forms, including task-related disagreements, intrapersonal conflicts within an individual, intergroup tensions among different groups, and interpersonal clashes between individuals. While task conflicts can be constructive by facilitating the exchange of ideas, conflicts can escalate into argumentative exchanges, disrupting harmony and tranquility within a group or organization.

The Thomas-Kilmann Conflict Mode Instrument (TKI) identifies five common conflict management styles, each reflecting a different approach to handling conflicts. Understanding these styles can help individuals effectively navigate conflicts and choose appropriate strategies for resolution. Here are the five conflict management styles according to the TKI:

Competing (Assertive, Uncooperative):

In the competing style, individuals assert their own concerns and objectives forcefully, often at the expense of others' interests.This approach prioritizes achieving one's own goals and may involve using power, authority, or persuasion to win the conflict.

Competing can be useful when quick decisions are needed or when standing up for important principles, but it may strain relationships and lead to resentment from others.

Collaborating (Assertive, Cooperative):

✓ Collaborating involves working together with others to find mutually beneficial solutions that address the concerns and interests of all parties.
✓ This style emphasizes open communication, active listening, and creative problem-solving to reach consensus.
✓ Collaboration is effective for resolving complex issues, building trust and teamwork, and maximizing long-term satisfaction, but it requires time and commitment from all involved.

Compromising (Moderately Assertive, Moderately Cooperative):

- ✓ Compromising aims to find a middle ground by making concessions and finding solutions that partially satisfy the concerns of all parties.
- ✓ Individuals using this style seek to meet halfway, accommodating some of their own needs while also considering the needs of others.
- ✓ Compromise can expedite conflict resolution and maintain relationships, but it may lead to suboptimal outcomes and unresolved underlying issues.

Avoiding (Unassertive, Uncooperative):

Avoiding involves sidestepping or postponing the conflict altogether, often by ignoring or withdrawing from the situation. This style may be used when the issue is trivial, when emotions are running high and need time to cool down, or when confrontation is perceived as futile or risky.Avoidance can provide temporary relief from conflict but may lead to unresolved tensions, missed opportunities for growth, and lingering resentment.

Accommodating (Unassertive, Cooperative):

Accommodating prioritizes maintaining harmony and preserving relationships by yielding to the needs and desires of others.

Individuals using this style are willing to sacrifice their own interests to accommodate the preferences or demands of others.Accommodation can build goodwill, reduce tensions, and promote cooperation, but it may also result in individuals neglecting their own needs and feeling taken advantage of.

Each conflict management style has its strengths and limitations, and the most appropriate approach depends on factors such as the nature of the conflict, the goals of the individuals involved, and the context in which the conflict arises. Effective conflict resolution often involves flexibly adapting one's approach and combining elements of different styles as needed to achieve the best possible outcome for all parties.

11. Teamwork

Teamwork is when individuals come together to pursue a shared objective, whether it's in a professional or personal setting. It's about collaboration, coordination, and mutual support. From lifting heavy furniture to tackling a project at work or playing a sport, teamwork can manifest in various ways.
Teamwork typically progresses through four stages: forming, storming, norming, and performing.

Forming:
In this initial stage, team members come together and get to know each other. They may be polite and cautious as they try to understand their roles, objectives, and how they fit into the team. There's

often a sense of excitement and anticipation as the team begins its journey.

Storming:

As the team starts working together, differences in opinions, personalities, and working styles may surface. This can lead to conflicts, disagreements, and challenges as individuals vie for their ideas to be heard. The storming stage can be tumultuous as the team navigates these tensions and tries to find common ground.

Norming:

In this stage, the team begins to resolve conflicts, establish norms, and develop cohesion. They start to understand and appreciate each other's strengths and weaknesses, and they work towards consensus on how to collaborate effectively. Norms around communication, decision-making, and problem-solving start to emerge, leading to greater stability within the team.

Performing:

Once the team has overcome the storming phase and established norms, they can focus on achieving their goals. In the performing stage, team members work together seamlessly, leveraging each other's strengths and supporting one another to accomplish tasks. There's a high level of trust, cooperation, and productivity as the team works towards its common objectives.

Effective teamwork thrives on motivation and inspiration. It involves managing conflicts constructively and leveraging individual strengths for collective success. Here are some signs that indicate a team is functioning well:

- The leadership style fosters fairness and open communication.
- Team members feel empowered to contribute their ideas and expertise.
- Feedback is welcomed and seen as an opportunity for growth.
- Mistakes are viewed as learning opportunities, with the team rallying to support each other.
- Patience is exercised, especially with those who are still developing their teamwork skills.

In essence, teamwork is about working together harmoniously, respecting each other's contributions, and striving towards a common goal. Natural examples are Honey bees and Ants.

12. Inspirational leadership

In today's fast-paced and competitive work environment, leadership transcends mere management; it embodies the ability to inspire, motivate, and uplift those around you toward collective success. Inspirational leadership, characterized by a positive influence on others and a relentless drive toward excellence, is not confined to the upper echelons of management. Rather, it is a quality that can be cultivated and practiced by individuals at any level of experience within an organization, from executives to entry-level employees. This essay explores the essence of inspirational leadership, highlighting its fundamental attributes and the profound impact it can have on teams and organizations.

The qualities of Inspirational leadership

the qualities of inspirational leadership presented in a point-wise format:

Passion and Purpose: Inspirational leaders are deeply passionate about their work and the vision they espouse. They infuse every action with a sense of purpose and meaning, inspiring others to share in their enthusiasm.

Visionary Leadership: They lead with vision and purpose, articulating a compelling vision of the future that resonates with team members and provides a roadmap for success.

Calm and Positive Attitude: Inspirational leaders remain composed and optimistic, even in the face of adversity and uncertainty, serving as a source of strength and stability for their team members.

Human Side: They show empathy and compassion toward their team members, taking the time to listen and understand their concerns, and offering support and guidance when needed.

Resilience: Inspirational leaders exhibit resilience in the face of challenges and setbacks, demonstrating fortitude and confidence in their ability to navigate difficulties.

Integrity: They uphold high ethical standards and act with honesty and transparency in all their interactions, earning the trust and respect of their team members.

Talent Development: Inspirational leaders are committed to developing talent within their team, providing mentorship, coaching, and opportunities for learning and growth.

Empathy and Emotional Intelligence: They possess empathy and emotional intelligence, enabling them to understand and connect with the emotions and experiences of others.

Motivation and Encouragement: They inspire and motivate others to unleash their full potential, providing encouragement and recognition for a job well done.

Recognition and Celebration: Inspirational leaders acknowledge and appreciate the contributions of their team members, celebrating milestones and achievements to reinforce positive behaviors and inspire others.

Leading by Example & Learn continiousely.

Chapter-5

Character Strengths and Virtue

*When wealth is lost, nothing is lost; when health is lost, something is lost; when character is lost, all is lost. —
Billy Graham.*

Character is the essence of who we are, reflecting our values, integrity, and moral fiber. It guides our actions, shapes our relationships, and influences our impact on the world.

A strong character is built on honesty, integrity, responsibility, compassion, and resilience. It fosters trust, respect, and authenticity in our interactions with others. Character defines our identity, shapes our reputation, and ultimately determines the legacy we leave behind.

In a world where integrity and ethical behavior are paramount, nurturing and cultivating good character is essential for personal growth, success, and contributing positively to society.Virtue is the embodiment of moral excellence and noble qualities that guide our thoughts, actions, and relationships. Rooted in principles such as honesty, compassion, integrity, and courage, virtue shapes our character and influences our behavior.

It is the foundation of ethical conduct, fostering trust, respect, and harmony in society. Practicing virtue leads to personal fulfillment, meaningful connections with others, and contributes to the greater good. By cultivating virtue, individuals cultivate their best selves and strive to make a positive impact on the world around them, creating a more just, compassionate, and harmonious society.

Dr.A.P.J Abdul Kalam story for Character and Virtues

Dr. APJ Abdul Kalam, affectionately known as the "Missile Man of India," was a renowned scientist, visionary leader, and the 11th President of India. His life journey is a testament to the power of perseverance, dedication, and the pursuit of excellence. Through his remarkable achievements and inspiring quotes, Dr. Kalam's character exemplified humility, wisdom, and a deep commitment to serving humanity.

Born on October 15, 1931, in Rameswaram, Tamil Nadu, Kalam hailed from a humble background. Despite facing financial constraints during his early years, he displayed exceptional academic talent and a keen interest in science and technology. After completing his education in aerospace engineering, Kalam joined India's defense research program, where he played a pivotal role in developing indigenous missile technology.One of Kalam's most significant achievements was his leadership in the development of India's first indigenous satellite launch vehicle, SLV-III, which successfully launched the Rohini satellite into space in 1980. This milestone marked India's entry into the league of space-faring nations and earned

Kalam widespread recognition for his contributions to the country's space program.

Throughout his illustrious career, Dr. Kalam held various prestigious positions, including Scientific Advisor to the Prime Minister and Secretary of the Defense Research and Development Organization (DRDO). However, it was his role as the President of India from 2002 to 2007 that catapulted him to the status of a national icon. As President, Kalam endeared himself to the public with his humility, accessibility, and dedication to youth empowerment and education.

Beyond his scientific and political achievements, Dr. Kalam's character was defined by his profound wisdom and humility. He was a deeply spiritual individual who believed in the power of education to transform lives and drive societal progress. Kalam was known for his simple lifestyle, humility, and unwavering commitment to serving others, regardless of their background or status. Dr. Kalam's life was also marked by his inspiring quotes, which continue to resonate with people around the world. Some of his most famous quotes include:

- "Dream, dream, dream. Dreams transform into thoughts, and thoughts result in action."
- "You have to dream before your dreams can come true."
- "If you want to shine like a sun, first burn like a sun."
- "Learning gives creativity, creativity leads to thinking, thinking provides knowledge, and knowledge makes you great."
- "Excellence is a continuous process, not an accident."

- *"All of us do not have equal talent. But, all of us have an equal opportunity to develop our talents."*

Dr. APJ Abdul Kalam's life and achievements serve as an inspiration to millions of people worldwide. His exemplary character, marked by humility, wisdom, and dedication to service, continues to be celebrated long after his passing. Through his remarkable journey and timeless words of wisdom, Kalam leaves behind a legacy that will inspire generations to come to dream, innovate, and work tirelessly towards a better future for all.

The concept of Character Strengths and Virtues (CSV)

Six fundamental virtues are prevalent across various cultures and can contribute to enhanced happiness when cultivated.

1. **Wisdom and Knowledge:** Creativity, curiosity, open-mindedness, love of learning, perspective, innovation, prudence
2. **Courage:** Bravery, persistence, vitality, zest
3. **Humanity:** Love, kindness, social intelligence
4. **Justice:** Citizenship, fairness, leadership, integrity, excellence
5. **Temperance:** Forgiveness and mercy, humility, self-control
6. **Transcendence:** Appreciation of beauty, gratitude, hope, humor, spirituality

Chapter-6

Positive Mindset

Positive thinking is a valuable tool that can help you overcome obstacles, deal with pain, and reach new goals." - Amy Morin

A positive mindset, characterized by optimism, resilience, and self-belief, offers numerous benefits across various aspects of life.

It can lead to improved mental and physical health outcomes, increased resilience in the face of challenges, greater happiness and life satisfaction. Enhanced relationships, boosted performance and productivity, better problem-solving skills, and even increased longevity. Overall, cultivating a positive mindset empowers individuals to navigate life's ups and downs with grace and optimism, ultimately leading to a happier and more fulfilling life.

Bumblee Bee Positive mind set creature :-

Buzz the bumblebee's story is a powerful example to the strength of a positive mindset. Despite facing scientific challenges that suggested he shouldn't be able to fly due to his heavy body and small wings, Buzz remained undeterred. Instead of dwelling on his limitations, he focused on his strengths and believed in his ability to overcome obstacles.

With unwavering determination, Buzz faced his fears and doubts head-on, refusing to let them hold him back. He knew that success was possible if he persisted, so he continued to push himself forward, even in the face of setbacks. Buzz's resilience allowed him to learn from his mistakes and grow stronger with each challenge he encountered.

His story serves as an inspiration to others, showing that with a positive mindset and a willingness to persevere, anything is achievable. Despite the odds, Buzz proved that belief in oneself can lead to extraordinary accomplishments, reminding us all of the power that lies within us when we choose to embrace positivity and determination.

Baby elephant negative mindset :-

The story of the elephant illustrates the power of mindset and the impact of past experiences on our behavior. Despite being incredibly strong, the elephant remains tied with a rope, unable to break free. This is not because the rope is stronger than the elephant, but because the elephant lacks a positive mindset.

As a baby elephant, it tries to break free from heavy chains but fails due to their weight. As it grows stronger, it could easily break free from the rope. However, the memory of its past failure holds it back. Even though it is now capable of breaking the rope, the elephant remains trapped by its own beliefs.

This story teaches us that our past experiences can sometimes limit us, even when we are capable of achieving more. It highlights the importance of having a positive mindset and overcoming self-imposed limitations. Just like the elephant, we have the strength to break free from our constraints if we believe in ourselves and our abilities

Positive Mindset functions :

A positive mindset, characterized by optimism, resilience, and self-belief, offers manifold benefits across various aspects of life:

- ✓ **Mental and Physical Health:** It reduces stress, anxiety, and depression, while also strengthening the immune system and lowering blood pressure.
- ✓ **Resilience:** Individuals adeptly navigate setbacks, viewing challenges as opportunities for growth.
- ✓ **Happiness and Satisfaction:** Positivity fosters increased levels of happiness and life satisfaction by enabling individuals to appreciate the present and focus on the good in their lives.
- ✓ **Relationships:** Positive individuals foster deeper social connections and more fulfilling interactions.
- ✓ **Performance:** Motivation, creativity, and productivity are boosted, leading to increased success in endeavors.
- ✓ **Problem-Solving:** Optimism facilitates clearer thinking, resulting in more effective problem-solving and decision-making.
- ✓ **Longevity:** Studies suggest a positive outlook correlates with a longer, healthier life due to the adoption of healthier habits and lifestyles.

In essence, cultivating a positive mindset empowers individuals to thrive in the face of adversity and lead fulfilling lives.

The positive mindset of Arunima Sinha

Arunima Sinha was a woman of remarkable courage and resilience, whose life story serves as an inspiration to millions around the world. Born with a passion for sports, she excelled as a national-level volleyball and football player in India. With dreams of serving her country, she aspired to join the paramilitary forces. However, her life took a tragic turn on April 12, 2011, when she faced a life-changing accident while traveling to Delhi.

On that fateful day, Arunima boarded the Padmavati Express train at Lucknow, intending to take an examination to join the Central Industrial Security Force (CISF). Little did she know that her journey would take a horrific turn. As the train chugged along its route, a group of hooligans attempted to rob her, pushing her out of the moving train in their bid to snatch her belongings. Unable to move, Arunima found herself lying on the railway track, helpless as an oncoming train ran over her leg below the knee.

The gruesome incident left Arunima with severe leg and pelvic injuries, resulting in the amputation of her leg to save her life. Despite the overwhelming challenges she faced, Arunima refused to be defined by her disability. With unwavering determination and inner strength, she embarked on a journey of healing and transformation.In the face of adversity, Arunima found the courage to pursue her dreams with even greater fervor. Inspired by the resilience of others, including cricketer Yuvraj Singh, who had battled cancer, she resolved to climb Mount Everest. With sheer grit and determination, she underwent rigorous training, excelling in a basic mountaineering course and overcoming numerous obstacles along the way.

In 2013, Arunima made history by becoming the first female amputee to conquer Mount Everest. Despite facing countless challenges and enduring grueling conditions, she reached the summit, defying all odds and inspiring millions with her indomitable spirit.Following her triumphant ascent of Mount Everest, Arunima's journey of adventure and exploration continued. She embarked on a mission to climb the highest peaks on every continent, setting her sights on Mount Vinson in Antarctica. In 2019, she achieved her goal, becoming the world's first female amputee to conquer Mount Vinson and completing her quest to climb the seven highest peaks on seven continents.

Throughout her extraordinary journey, Arunima has not only overcome physical obstacles but also championed social causes. She is dedicated to promoting sports and empowering individuals with disabilities, aiming to open a free sports academy for the underprivileged and disabled. Her selfless efforts and unwavering commitment to serving others have earned her numerous accolades, including the Padma Shri, India's fourth-highest civilian award.

Arunima Sinha's story is a testament to the power of resilience, determination, and the human spirit. Despite facing unimaginable hardships, she has emerged as a beacon of hope and inspiration, showing the world that no obstacle is insurmountable for those who dare to dream and persevere against all odds. Her journey serves as a reminder that with courage, perseverance, and a positive mindset, anything is possible.

Chapter-7
Wellbeing

"The first wealth is health."~ Ralph Waldo Emerson

Well-being, also referred to as wellness, prudential value, prosperity, or quality of life, pertains to what holds intrinsic value for an individual. It encompasses what is ultimately beneficial and in the self-interest of that person. Well-being can encompass both positive and negative aspects, with its positive sense often juxtaposed with ill-being as its opposite. The term "subjective well-being" describes individuals' experiences and evaluations of their lives, typically assessed through self-reported measures obtained from questionnaires.

A Story of Positive wellbeing

Once upon a time, there was a cozy glass house nestled near a sparkling lake. The house belonged to a kind father and his young son. At first, the boy loved his new home, especially because he had a lovely view of the shimmering lake from his bedroom window. He would gaze out at the water, feeling happy and content.
But as days went by, the boy started to notice something. He thought the water in the lake looked dirty and murky. He complained to his father, saying, "Dad, why is the lake so dirty? I can't enjoy the view anymore."

The father listened to his son's concerns and decided to do something about it. He took a cloth and some cleaning supplies and began to wash the window glasses, both from the inside and outside of the house. The boy watched as his father worked diligently, wondering what difference it would make.

To the boy's surprise, when his father finished cleaning the windows, the view of the lake was breathtakingly beautiful once again. The water sparkled in the sunlight, and the surrounding trees looked greener and more vibrant.

The boy realized that the lake hadn't changed at all. It was still the same beautiful place it had always been. It was his perspective that had changed because of the dirty windows.

The father smiled at his son and said, "Sometimes, we see things differently depending on how clear our minds are. Just like cleaning the window made the view better, having a positive mindset can make the world seem brighter and more beautiful."

From that day on, the boy remembered his father's words whenever he felt tempted to judge others. He understood that having a clear and positive outlook on life could make all the difference in how he saw the world around him.

Various forms of well-being

Well-being can manifest in various forms, encompassing both physical and mental aspects of life. Here are some examples of well-being:

Physical Well-being: This refers to the state of the body and its ability to function optimally. Examples include:

- ❖ Being physically fit and active through regular exercise.
- ❖ Maintaining a healthy weight and balanced diet.
- ❖ Getting enough quality sleep each night.
- ❖ Being free from illness or chronic health conditions.

Emotional Well-being: Emotional well-being relates to one's ability to manage emotions, cope with stress, and maintain a positive outlook on life. Examples include:

- ❖ Feeling content and satisfied with life overall.
- ❖ Having healthy ways to cope with stress, such as meditation, deep breathing exercises, or seeking support from others.
- ❖ Being able to recognize and express a wide range of emotions, both positive and negative, in a healthy manner.
- ❖ Having a sense of resilience and bouncing back from setbacks or adversity.

Social Well-being: Social well-being involves having fulfilling and meaningful relationships with others, as well as feeling connected to a larger community. Examples include:

- ❖ Having close and supportive relationships with family, friends, and peers.
- ❖ Feeling a sense of belonging and acceptance within social groups or communities.
- ❖ Engaging in regular social activities and interactions that bring joy and fulfillment.
- ❖ Having a strong support network to turn to in times of need.

Intellectual Well-being: Intellectual well-being pertains to the stimulation of the mind, ongoing learning, and the pursuit of knowledge and creativity. Examples include:

- ❖ Engaging in lifelong learning activities, such as reading, taking courses, or attending workshops.
- ❖ Pursuing hobbies and interests that challenge and stimulate the mind, such as puzzles, games, or creative arts.
- ❖ Setting and achieving intellectual goals, such as mastering a new skill or acquiring expertise in a particular area.
- ❖ Being open-minded and receptive to new ideas, perspectives, and experiences.

Spiritual Well-being: Spiritual well-being involves finding meaning, purpose, and connection to something greater than oneself. Examples include:

- ❖ Engaging in spiritual practices or rituals that promote inner peace, reflection, and mindfulness, such as meditation, prayer, or yoga.
- ❖ Exploring existential questions about life, death, and the universe and finding personal meaning and fulfillment in those inquiries.
- ❖ Feeling a sense of awe, wonder, and reverence for the natural world and the mysteries of existence.
- ❖ Finding alignment with one's values, beliefs, and sense of purpose in life.

These examples illustrate the multifaceted nature of well-being and highlight the importance of nurturing various aspects of life to achieve overall health and happiness.

Wellbeing in Positive Psychology :-

Well-being holds a central position within the realm of positive psychology. Positive psychology focuses on eudaimonia, often described as "the good life," which involves contemplating what aspects of life are most valuable and contribute to a fulfilling existence. While positive psychologists may not offer a precise definition of the good life, they generally concur that it entails living happily, engaging fully, and finding meaning in life's experiences.

Martin Seligman, a prominent figure in positive psychology, characterizes "the good life" as utilizing one's unique strengths on a daily basis to cultivate genuine happiness and abundant satisfaction. This perspective emphasizes the importance of leveraging personal strengths to enhance well-being and achieve a fulfilling life.

Carol Ryff Six factor model of Psychological wellbeing :-

The Six-Factor Model of Psychological Well-Being, developed by Carol Ryff, is a multidimensional framework that draws inspiration from Aristotle's concept of eudaimonia, or "the good life." This model identifies six key factors that contribute to an individual's overall psychological well-being. Each factor encompasses smaller subsections that reflect different aspects of well-being:

1. Self Acceptance
2. Personal Growth
3. Purpose in Life
4. Environment Mastery
5. Autonomy
6. Positive relations with others.

Self-acceptance:

This factor relates to an individual's ability to accept and embrace themselves as they are, including their strengths and weaknesses. It involves having a positive self-image and feeling satisfied with oneself.

Personal growth:

Personal growth refers to the ongoing process of self-improvement, development, and realization of one's potential. It involves setting and achieving goals, learning new skills, and adapting to life's challenges.

Purpose in life:

Having a sense of purpose or meaning in life is essential for psychological well-being. This factor encompasses feeling that one's life has direction and meaning, and that their actions contribute to something larger than themselves.

Environmental mastery:

Environmental mastery refers to an individual's ability to effectively manage and navigate their environment. This includes feeling competent in handling life's demands, feeling in control of one's surroundings, and being able to adapt to change.

Autonomy:

Autonomy relates to the sense of independence and self-determination that individuals have in their lives. It involves making choices that align with one's values and desires, and feeling a sense of control over one's own destiny.

Positive relations with others:

This factor emphasizes the importance of meaningful and fulfilling relationships with others. It involves having strong social connections, experiencing empathy and compassion, and feeling supported by others.

Overall, the Six-Factor Model of Psychological Well-Being provides a comprehensive framework for understanding the various dimensions of psychological well-being and how they contribute to overall life satisfaction and fulfillment.

Chapter-8

Interpersonal Relationship

"The quality of your life is the quality of your relationships." - Tony Robbins

Interpersonal relationships refer to the social connections or affiliations between individuals, encompassing various degrees of intimacy, self-disclosure, duration, reciprocity, and power distribution. This concept closely aligns with social relations, which are fundamental units of analysis in the social sciences.

These relationships manifest in diverse contexts such as family, kinship, friendship, love, marriage, business, employment, clubs, neighborhoods, ethical values, support, and solidarity. They are governed by legal, customary, or mutual agreements and serve as the foundation of social groups and societies. Interpersonal relationships emerge when people interact or engage with each other within specific social settings, relying on fair and reciprocal compromises to thrive.

Positive learning story about Interpersonal relationship

The story of the interpersonal relationship between our legs beautifully illustrates the importance of coordination and collaboration in achieving progress. Like two close friends, our legs work together in perfect harmony, each playing its part in the act of walking or running. Just as in any healthy relationship, there is a natural give and take between them.

Sometimes the right leg takes the lead, while other times it's the left leg. But regardless of who leads, they always support each other, moving forward in sync. This coordination is essential for visible progress in walking or running. Similarly, in life, positive psychology emphasizes the significance of interpersonal relationships and teamwork. Just as our legs rely on each other to move forward, individuals thrive when they collaborate, support, and work together towards common goals. It is through this interconnectedness and mutual support that true progress and success are achieved

How to Improve Interpersonal relationships

Just like a lion uses its strength to catch other animals for food, it also uses the same strength to carry its cubs safely. When hunting, a lion uses its teeth and jaws to catch and kill prey, but when it's caring for its cubs, it gently lifts them with the same teeth and carries them to a safe place. Even though the lion uses the same teeth and jaws for both purposes, its actions are very different. In the same way, our interpersonal skills are like the lion's actions. We might use the same skills to communicate with others, but the way we use them can vary depending on the situation. For example, we might use our communication skills to resolve conflicts or to build friendships. Just like the lion adapts its actions based on the situation, we too can adapt our interpersonal skills to meet the needs of different social situations.

Improving interpersonal relationships involves various strategies aimed at enhancing communication, understanding, and mutual respect. Here are some effective ways to improve interpersonal relationships:

- ❖ Practice active listening, empathy, and assertiveness. Be open, honest, and respectful in your interactions with others. Clarify misunderstandings and express your thoughts and feelings constructively.
- ❖ ***Empathy:***,Put yourself in the other person's shoes and try to understand their perspective, feelings, and needs. Show empathy by acknowledging their emotions and validating their experiences.
- ❖ ***Conflict resolution:*** Learn effective conflict resolution skills, such as negotiation, compromise, and problem-solving. Address conflicts calmly and constructively, focusing on finding mutually acceptable solutions.
- ❖ ***Boundaries:*** Establish and respect personal boundaries in relationships. Communicate your boundaries clearly and assertively, and respect the boundaries of others. Boundaries help maintain healthy and balanced relationships.

- ❖ ***Respect:*** Treat others with kindness, courtesy, and consideration. Respect their opinions, beliefs, and choices, even if they differ from your own. Show appreciation and gratitude for their contributions and efforts.
- ❖ ***Trust:*** Build trust through honesty, reliability, and consistency in your words and actions. Be trustworthy and maintain confidentiality when necessary. Trust forms the foundation of strong interpersonal relationships.
- ❖ ***Quality time:*** Invest time and effort in nurturing relationships through meaningful interactions and shared experiences. Spend quality time together, engage in activities you both enjoy, and create lasting memories.
- ❖ ***Forgiveness:*** Practice forgiveness and let go of past grievances or resentments. Accept that everyone makes mistakes and focus on moving forward positively. Forgiveness promotes healing and strengthens relationships.
- ❖ Offer support and encouragement to others during challenging times. Show empathy, compassion, and willingness to help when needed. Be a reliable source of emotional and practical support.
- ❖ ***Self-awareness:*** Reflect on your own behavior, communication style, and interpersonal skills. Identify areas for improvement and work on developing self-awareness, emotional intelligence, and social competence.

Chapter-9

Flow or Engagement

"Flow is the mental state of operation in which a person performing an activity is fully immersed in a feeling of energized focus, full involvement, and enjoyment in the process of the activity." - Mihaly Csikszentmihalyi

Engagement', in terms of positive psychology, describes really focused and enjoying what you're doing. Another name for this is 'flow' Engagement. It is when you're really focused and enjoying what you're doing. You feel totally into it, like you're in a special zone. It's like time flies because you're so absorbed in what you're doing. It happens when what you're doing matches your skills and is just challenging enough. You need to concentrate a lot to get into this state. People use flow to deal with stress and anxiety by doing something they're good at and enjoy.

Motivation example:

Flow is an individual experience and the idea behind flow originated from the sports-psychology theory about an Individual Zone of Optimal Functioning.

*In 1938, a 28-year-old soldier named **Karoly Takacs** from the Hungarian Army was one of the best pistol shooters in the world. He had won many championships and was expected to win gold at the 1940*

Olympics. But just before the Olympics, a grenade exploded in his right hand during training, destroying his hand and his dream of competing.

After a month in the hospital, instead of feeling sorry for himself, Takacs decided to keep pursuing his Olympic dream. Even though he couldn't use his right hand anymore, he decided to learn to shoot with his left hand. Despite not being left-handed, he practiced hard and stayed focused on his goal. He believed that having the right attitude and determination was more important than just having the skills.

For months, Takacs practiced shooting alone, without telling anyone. He didn't want to hear discouraging words from others. In the spring of 1939, he surprised everyone by competing in the Hungarian National Pistol Shooting Championship and winning.Even though the 1940 and 1944 Olympics were canceled due to World War II, Takacs continued to train. In 1948, at the age of 38, he qualified for the London Olympics and won the gold medal by defeating the reigning world champion and setting a new world record. Four years later, he won another gold medal at the 1952 Helsinki Olympics.

After he finished his shooting career, Takács became a coach. He trained a Hungarian shooter named Szilárd Kun, who went on to win the silver medal at the 1952 Summer Olympics. Takács eventually retired from the army with the rank of lieutenant colonel."

The most memorable moments in life don't typically come from times of passivity or relaxation. Instead, they often arise when we push ourselves to the brink, either physically or mentally, in pursuit of challenging and meaningful goals. Embrace whatever comes your way, allowing your mind to remain unfettered and focused. By accepting and staying centered in every moment, you'll reach the pinnacle of experience.

How to improve Flow sets ?

Intrinsic Motivation will help to improve flow sets. Choose activities that you genuinely enjoy and find meaningful. Flow is more likely to occur when you're intrinsically motivated and derive pleasure from the process itself, rather than just the outcome.

Dashrath Manjhi, known as the "Mountain Man" of India, was an impoverished laborer from Gehlaur village in Bihar. His village was isolated due to a massive mountain that obstructed access to essential services like healthcare and education. In 1959, his wife, Falguni Devi, died from injuries because the nearest doctor was 55 kilometers away, accessible only by traveling around the mountain. Motivated by this tragedy, Manjhi vowed to carve a path through the mountain.

Starting in 1960 with just a hammer, chisel, and crowbar, he faced grueling physical labor, social ridicule, and a lack of support. For 22 years, Manjhi chipped away at the mountain, completing the path in 1982. His 110-meter-long, 9.1-meter-wide, and 7.6-meter-deep road reduced the travel distance between the Atri and Wazirganj blocks from 55 to 15 kilometers, greatly improving access to services for the villagers.

Though he worked in obscurity, Manjhi's achievement eventually gained recognition. The government of Bihar named the road after him, and his story was made into the 2015 biographical film "Manjhi - The Mountain Man." Dashrath Manjhi's determination and perseverance continue to inspire many, demonstrating that with unwavering resolve and hard work, even the most daunting obstacles can be overcome.

Passion challenge and skill engage in activities that are challenging enough to require your full attention and skill level, but not so difficult that they become overwhelming. Striking the right balance between challenge and skill is essential for entering flow.

Florence Chadwick was a renowned American long-distance swimmer known for her many swimming achievements. One of her most notable attempts occurred on July 4, 1952, when she tried to swim the 21 miles from Catalina Island to the California coast. Despite her extensive experience, the cold sea, dense fog, and presence of sharks posed significant challenges. After nearly 15 hours of swimming, she gave up, unable to see the shore and doubting her progress. She later discovered she was less than a mile from her goal. This experience highlighted the importance of perseverance and maintaining faith in the face of unclear paths.

Two months later, Chadwick successfully completed the swim, demonstrating her determination and resilience. Her story is an inspiring example of overcoming setbacks through renewed effort and focus

Flow will helpful to stop overthinking and micro management of others.

Chapter-10
Optimisam

Optimism is the faith that leads to achievement. Nothing can be done without hope and confidence." - Helen Keller

Optimism is a mindset marked by hope and belief in success and a bright future. Those who embrace optimism see challenges as opportunities for growth or short-lived obstacles. Even on tough days, optimists hold onto the belief that "tomorrow is likely to be better," finding solace in the prospect of brighter days ahead.

Optimism acts as a magnet, attracting happiness and positivity into one's life. Like a magnetic force, a positive outlook on life draws in good things and good people. When individuals maintain optimism, they radiate a contagious energy that uplifts those around them. This positivity not only enhances personal well-being but also creates a favorable environment for success and fulfillment.

The concept of the glass being "half empty" or "half full" reflects by Martin Seligman's Glass Half Full, two contrasting perspectives: pessimism and optimism.When someone sees the glass as half empty, they adopt a pessimistic outlook, focusing on what is lacking or missing. They may dwell on the negatives, anticipate failure, and feel discouraged by challenges.

This mindset can lead to feelings of dissatisfaction, anxiety, and a sense of hopelessness.Conversely, viewing the glass as half full signifies an optimistic perspective. Optimists focus on what is present and see potential for growth and improvement. They approach situations with a positive attitude, embrace challenges as opportunities for growth, and maintain hope for the future. This mindset fosters resilience, gratitude, and a sense of empowerment.

While pessimism tends to hinder progress and diminish well-being, optimism cultivates resilience and enhances overall quality of life. Ultimately, whether the glass is half empty or half full depends on one's perspective and mindset, highlighting the profound impact of attitude on perception and experience.

Signs of Optimisam :-

- ❖ You hold a belief that positive outcomes await in the future.
- ❖ You maintain an expectation that things will ultimately resolve in a favorable manner.
- ❖ You possess a sense of confidence in your ability to overcome life's obstacles and achieve success.
- ❖ You perceive the future as filled with promise and potential.
- ❖ You recognize that even adversities can yield positive outcomes or valuable lessons.

- ❖ You view challenges or setbacks as opportunities for personal growth and development.
- ❖ You express gratitude for the blessings and positive aspects of your life.
- ❖ You actively seek ways to capitalize on opportunities and maximize their potential.
- ❖ You maintain a positive attitude towards yourself and others, fostering supportive relationships.
- ❖ You take ownership of your mistakes while refraining from dwelling on them excessively.
- ❖ You refuse to allow one negative experience to tarnish your overall optimism and expectations for the future.

Explanatory theory style explaining practical approaches

In 2009, Brian Acton faced a series of rejections that would later turn into a legendary tale of perseverance and triumph. At that time, he applied for jobs at social media giants Twitter and Facebook but was met with disappointment as both companies turned him down.

Facebook turned me down. It was a great opportunity to connect with some fantastic people. Looking forward to life's next adventure.

8:14 PM - 3 Aug 2009

Despite these setbacks, Acton remained undeterred and continued to pursue his passion for technology and innovation. Alongside his friend Jan Koum, he co-founded WhatsApp, a messaging app designed to provide a simple and efficient way for people to communicate.WhatsApp initially faced challenges and struggled to gain traction in a crowded market. However, Acton and Koum refused to give up on their vision. They remained dedicated to improving the app and providing users with a reliable messaging platform.

Their persistence paid off when WhatsApp began to gain popularity, quickly becoming one of the most widely used messaging apps worldwide. In 2014, Facebook recognized the potential of WhatsApp and acquired the company for a staggering $19 billion, marking one of the largest acquisitions in tech history.

Acton's journey from rejection to success serves as a powerful example of the importance of perseverance and optimism in the face of adversity. Despite facing setbacks and initial failures, he remained committed to his goals and ultimately achieved remarkable success.

His story serves as inspiration for job seekers and entrepreneurs alike, reminding us that with determination, hard work, and a positive mindset, anything is possible. Brian Acton's resilience and optimism have cemented his place as a legend in the world of tech and entrepreneurship.

Whether you tend to be more optimistic or pessimistic can often be explained by how you interpret the events in your life.Your explanatory style, or how you explain events, plays a big role.

There are three parts to this:

1. Stable vs. Unstable: Do things change over time, or do they stay the same?
2. Global vs. Local: Is an event just about one part of your life, or does it affect everything?
3. Internal vs. External: Do you think events happen because of you, or because of outside forces?

Optimists explain good things as their own doing (internal), thinking they'll keep happening (stable) and affect other parts of their life too (global). They see bad things as not their fault (external), and think they won't happen again (unstable) and only affect that one part of their life (local).

For example, if an optimist gets a promotion, they'll likely think it's because they're good at their job and expect more good things in the future. If they don't get the promotion, they might blame it on temporary issues and believe they'll do better next time.

Pessimists see things the opposite way. They think bad events are their fault (internal), expect more bad things to happen (stable), and think it affects everything (global). They see good events as just luck (local), caused by things out of their control (external), and unlikely to happen again (unstable).

For instance, if a pessimist gets a promotion, they might worry it's a one-time thing and fear more pressure. If they don't get promoted, they might blame their lack of skills and expect to be passed over again.

Difference between Optimistic and Pessimistic

Aspect	Optimistic	Pessimistic
Outlook on the future	Believes in positive outcomes and opportunities	Expects negative outcomes and dwells on potential failures
Response to setbacks	Views setbacks as temporary and learning experiences	Sees setbacks as permanent and indicative of personal shortcomings
Attribution of events	Attributes success to own abilities or external factors	Attributes failure to personal deficiencies or bad luck
Approach to challenges	Views challenges as opportunities for growth	Views challenges as insurmountable obstacles
General attitude	Maintains a positive and hopeful demeanor	Tends to have a negative and pessimistic outlook
Coping mechanisms	Uses positive coping strategies and seeks solutions	May engage in avoidance or resignation behaviors
Impact on well-being	Often experiences higher levels of happiness and satisfaction	May experience higher levels of stress and dissatisfaction
Response to criticism	Accepts criticism constructively and seeks improvement	Takes criticism personally and may become defensive

How to practice Optimisam :-

✓ Mindfulness -Stay present in the moment and focus on what you can control rather than worrying about the future or dwelling on the past. Mindfulness techniques such as meditation or deep breathing exercises can help you stay grounded and appreciative of the present.

✓ Gratitude: Take time each day to reflect on the things you're grateful for. Keeping a gratitude journal or simply listing things you appreciate can help shift your focus towards the positive aspects of your life.

✓ Positive self-talk: Pay attention to your inner dialogue and challenge negative thoughts with more optimistic ones. Replace self-criticism with affirmations and reminders of your strengths and past successes.

✓ Focus on solutions: When faced with challenges or setbacks, approach them as opportunities for growth rather than insurmountable obstacles. Look for ways to problem-solve and learn from your experiences rather than getting discouraged.

✓ Surround yourself with positivity: Spend time with supportive friends and family who uplift you and share your optimistic outlook. Limit exposure to negative influences such as pessimistic media or toxic relationships.

✓ Practice resilience: Cultivate resilience by embracing setbacks as learning opportunities and bouncing back from adversity with newfound strength and determination.

✓ Set realistic goals: Set achievable goals for yourself and celebrate your progress along the way. Break larger goals into smaller, manageable steps to maintain motivation and momentum.

✓ Stay optimistic in the face of uncertainty: Embrace uncertainty as a natural part of life and maintain faith in your ability to navigate challenges and adapt to changing circumstances.

By incorporating these practices into your daily life, you can gradually train your brain to adopt a more optimistic outlook and experience greater overall happiness and well-being.

Cognitive Restructring :-

Cognitive restructuring is a technique to become more optimistic by changing negative thinking patterns. Here's how it works:

Identify triggers: Recognize situations that make you feel negative.Example: If you feel anxious before a test, the test itself might be a trigger.

Assess feelings: Understand how you're feeling in that moment.Example: Before the test, you might feel nervous or worried.

Recognize negative thoughts: Notice the negative thoughts you have in response to the situation.Example: You might think, "I'm going to fail this test."

Review evidence: Look at evidence that supports or refutes your negative thoughts.Example: You remember past tests you've passed and how much you've studied.

Focus on facts: Concentrate on the objective facts and replace negative thoughts with positive ones.Example: Instead of thinking you'll fail, remind yourself that you've studied hard and have passed tests before.

Impact of Optimisam

Optimism has a significant impact on mental and physical well-being, offering various advantages:

- ❖ Better Health
- ❖ Optimistic individuals tend to perform better in various fields.
- ❖ Emotional Healthnvolves reframing thought processes well-being.
- ❖ Optimism also improves the quality of life for individuals facing illnesses
- ❖ Optimists experience less stress than pessimists. They believe in their abilities and see setbacks as minor hurdles to overcome.

Optimisam in Theraphy

Optimism is integral to therapy, enhancing clients' resilience and coping skills while instilling hope and empowerment in challenging circumstances.Therapists employ various techniques such as empathetic communication, group activities, and role-play to integrate optimism into therapy sessions.

Optimistic interventions are effective in addressing psychological conditions characterized by negative thinking and distress, such as major depression and postpartum depression.

For individuals experiencing trauma-related disorders like PTSD, fostering optimism helps envision a future beyond traumatic experiences and facilitates healing.

Chapter-11

Resilience

"Resilience is not what happens to you. It's how you react to, respond to, and recover from what happens to you." - Jeffrey Gitomer

Resilience means being able to bounce back from tough situations.Resilience involves the capacity to recover and bounce back from adversities and setbacks. It plays a crucial role in helping individuals deal with various problems and overcome trauma.

Do not judge me by my successes, judge me by how many times I fell down and got back up again."—Nelson Mandela

Once upon a time, people were treated differently based on the color of their skin. Whites often received better treatment, while blacks faced discrimination in various aspects of life. This racial inequality was widespread under British colonial rule, with South Africa experiencing some of the worst forms of segregation.In South Africa, the majority of the population was black, yet they faced economic hardship and social injustice.

Laws enforced by the National Party government in 1948 further entrenched racial segregation, with separate living areas and public services for blacks and whites. However, the persistence of individuals like Nelson Mandela eventually led to the end of these discriminatory practices.Born on July 18, 1918, in South Africa, Nelson Mandela grew up witnessing the injustices of apartheid. Despite facing personal tragedies, such as the death of his *father when he was just 12, Mandela pursued education and activism. He attended Healdtown College, where he began his fight against racial discrimination alongside lifelong friend Oliver Tambo.*

Mandela's involvement in the African National Congress (ANC) marked the beginning of his anti-apartheid movement. Despite facing persecution, including imprisonment and charges of treason, Mandela remained resilient. His commitment to nonviolent resistance, inspired by Mahatma Gandhi, eventually led to his release from prison in 1990.

Following his release, Mandela played a pivotal role in South Africa's transition to democracy. In 1994, he became the country's first black president, ushering in an era of equality and unity. Mandela's contributions earned him global recognition, including the Bharat Ratna and Nobel Peace Prize.

In conclusion, Nelson Mandela's life epitomizes resilience and perseverance in the face of adversity. His dedication to justice and equality continues to inspire people worldwide, earning him the title of "African Gandhi" and leaving a lasting legacy of hope and freedom. Resilience entails recognizing that life presents challenges which cannot always be avoided. However, individuals can cultivate resilience by remaining open, flexible, and adaptable to change.

Success represents the 1% of your work which results from the 99% that is called failure- Honda

Soichiro Honda's journey is a testament to resilience and determination. Despite facing adversity during World War II when his factory was bombed not once, but twice, Honda refused to give up. Instead of succumbing to defeat, he saw an opportunity for innovation.With a vision to create something new, Honda decided to combine a bicycle with a small motor, giving birth to the concept of a motorized scooter. Despite initial challenges, Honda persevered, and his scooter soon became a sensation, particularly in the United States.

Through his resilience and ability to bounce back from setbacks, Soichiro Honda not only built a successful automobile empire but also left behind a legacy of perseverance and ingenuity. His famous quotes of Bounceback

- ✓ The value of life can be measured by how many times your soul has been deeply stirred."
- ✓ "Success is 99% failure."
- ✓ "Instead of being afraid of the challenge and failure, be afraid of avoiding the challenge and doing nothing."
- ✓ "The power of dreams is that they can pull you forward and make them real."
- ✓ "The most disastrous thing that you can ever learn is your first success."
- ✓ "Without racing, there is no Honda."
- ✓ "I want to be remembered as someone who contributed to motor racing."
- ✓ "Action without philosophy is a lethal weapon; philosophy without action is worthless."
- ✓ "The value of life can be measured by how many times your soul has been deeply stirred."

Resilient individuals harness their inner strength to cope and rebound from challenges, including major traumas like job loss, financial difficulties, illness, relationship issues, or the loss of a loved one. They draw upon their resilience to navigate through difficult times and emerge stronger.

Resilience is like a mighty fortress built on the foundation of strength, persistence, and tenacity. It embodies the potency to withstand adversity and the perseverance to endure challenges. Like a sturdy tree rooted deeply in the ground, resilience demonstrates power and stubbornness against the storms of life. It is fortified by fortitude, doggedness, and grit, refusing to yield in the face of adversity.

Margaret Thatcher has quoted "You may have to fight a battle more than once to win it."

With unyielding obstinacy and tenaciousness, resilience stands tall like an iron pillar, unwavering and unbreakable. It possesses the backbone and sand to weather the toughest of storms, displaying obdurateness and obstinateness against all odds. Resilience thrives on autonomy, freedom, and self-reliance, embracing independence and self-sufficiency. It is fueled by self-determination, self-support, and self-dependence, ensuring self-subsistence even in the harshest of conditions to Bounceback.

Examples Traits of resilience in action include:

First, think. Second, dream. Third, believe. And finally, dare.- Walt Disney

Walt Disney, the visionary behind iconic characters like Mickey Mouse and Donald Duck, is synonymous with creativity and imagination. However, his path to success was paved with numerous setbacks and failures.Disney's first venture, Laugh-O-Gram, ended in bankruptcy, leaving him financially devastated. Undeterred by this setback, Disney persevered, determined to bring his creative vision to life. Despite facing numerous rejections, he refused to abandon his dreams. Then he quoted "All the adversity I've had in my life, all my troubles and obstacles, have strengthened me... You may not realize it when it happens, but a kick in the teeth may be the best thing in the world for you"

It wasn't until five years later that Disney's perseverance paid off. With unwavering determination and a relentless work ethic, he introduced the world to Mickey Mouse, a character that would change the course of animation history. All our dreams can come true, if we have the courage to pursue them.Although Mickey Mouse initially faced rejection from potential distributors, Disney remained undeterred. He took matters into his own hands, borrowing money to produce a series of cartoons featuring Mickey. The rest, as they say, is history.Disney's resilience and refusal to give up in the face of adversity ultimately led to the creation of the Walt Disney Company, one of the most beloved entertainment conglomerates in the world. His story serves as a powerful reminder that failure is not the end but rather a stepping stone to success. He belives " "First, think. Second, dream. Third, believe. And finally, dare."

- ***Taking a positive perspective:*** Instead of dwelling on negative aspects, resilient individuals try to see the silver lining in situations, focusing on the potential for growth and improvement.
- ***Viewing challenges as learning opportunities:*** Resilient individuals approach challenges as opportunities to learn and develop new skills, rather than as insurmountable obstacles.
- ***Regulating emotions:*** Resilient individuals effectively manage their emotions, expressing their feelings in appropriate ways and using coping strategies to stay calm and composed.
- ***Focusing on controllable factors:*** Resilient individuals concentrate on aspects of a situation that they can control, rather than fixating on elements beyond their influence.
- ***Recognizing cognitive distortions:*** Resilient individuals are aware of cognitive distortions—such as catastrophizing or black-and-white thinking—and challenge these false perceptions to maintain a realistic perspective.
- ***Reframing negative thoughts:*** Resilient individuals actively work to reframe negative thoughts into more realistic and positive ones, fostering a mindset of optimism and resilience.

For instance, consider a scenario where someone gets stuck in traffic on the way to work. A resilient individual might choose to focus on the lesson learned (leaving earlier in the future), manage their stress through relaxation techniques, and maintain a positive outlook by reminding themselves of their past punctuality and understanding employers.

Types of Resilience in Practical life :-

Resilience encompasses various types, each influencing how individuals cope with life's challenges. Here are the four main types of resilience:

1. Physical Resilience
2. Psychological Resilience
3. Emotional Reilience
4. Social Resilence

Physical Resilience: This type of resilience involves how the body responds to and recovers from physical demands, illnesses, and injuries. For instance, someone who regularly exercises, eats a balanced diet, and gets enough sleep is likely to have better physical resilience. **An example** of physical resilience is when a person recovers from an illness or injury and returns to their normal activities.

Psychological Resilience: Mental resilience refers to the ability to adapt to change and uncertainty, remaining calm and flexible during difficult situations. Individuals with mental resilience use their inner strength to solve problems and stay hopeful amidst setbacks. **An example** of mental resilience is when a person faces a sudden change in their work environment and manages to adjust their plans and continue working effectively.

Emotional Resilience: Emotional resilience involves regulating emotions during times of stress and maintaining optimism in the face of adversity. Resilient individuals are aware of their emotions and can manage them effectively. **An example** of emotional resilience is when someone experiences a setback in their personal life but remains positive and optimistic about the future.

Social Resilience: Social resilience, or community resilience, refers to the ability of groups to recover from difficult situations by coming together and supporting each other. It involves building strong social connections and working collaboratively to overcome challenges. **An example** of social resilience is when a community comes together to rebuild after a natural disaster, providing support and resources to those in need.

How to build effective Reslience (Bounceback)

Resilience refers Bounceback to one's ability to effectively navigate and recover from life's challenges. It can determine how well one handles pressure and maintains composure in difficult situations. Resilient individuals typically maintain a positive mindset and manage stress more adeptly.While resilience may come naturally to some, research suggests that it can also be cultivated through learned behaviors. Whether currently facing adversity or preparing for future challenges, resilience can be developed by:

- ❖ Finding purpose and meaning in life.
- ❖ Cultivating self-belief and confidence.
- ❖ Building a supportive social network.
- ❖ Embracing change and adapting to new circumstances.

- ❖ Maintaining an optimistic outlook on life.
- ❖ Prioritizing self-care and well-being.
- ❖ Developing problem-solving skills to tackle challenges effectively.
- ❖ Setting and pursuing meaningful goals.
- ❖ Taking proactive steps and initiative.
- ❖ Committing to continuous skill development and growth over time.

Characterstics of Resilience :-

Pain is temporary. It may last for a minute, or an hour, or a day, or even a year. But eventually, it will subside and something else will take its place. If I quit, however, it will last forever."— Eric Thomas

Britney Spears is an American singer, songwriter, dancer, and actress who rose to fame in the late 1990s and early 2000s. Britney Spears faced some tough times in the public eye, especially when she lost custody of her children to her ex-husband Kevin Federline. She was involved in incidents that got a lot of attention, like shaving her head in public, driving with her son on her lap, and confronting paparazzi with an umbrella.Things got really tough for her, and she ended up in a psychiatric hospital in January 2008. But just five days later, she was released and didn't let that stop her. Instead, she came back stronger than ever.

After her release, she didn't give up on her career. She released her sixth album and showed the world that she was ready to bounce back. From there on, her career only got better, and she proved that she could overcome challenges and come out on top. Britney Spears' story is a powerful reminder that no matter what obstacles you face, you can always bounce back and achieve success. Despite these challenges, she remains a significant figure in the entertainment industry and continues to inspire fans worldwide with her music and resilience.

The five fundamental characteristics of resilience are:

1. Problem-solving skills: Resilient individuals possess the ability to effectively identify and tackle challenges, finding practical solutions to overcome obstacles.
2. Strong social connections: Resilience is reinforced by supportive relationships with family, friends, and community members, providing emotional encouragement and practical assistance during tough times.
3. Survivor mentality: Resilient individuals maintain a positive mindset, viewing setbacks as temporary and surmountable, and embracing an attitude of perseverance and determination.
4. Emotional regulation: Resilience involves the capacity to manage and regulate emotions effectively, staying calm and composed even in the face of adversity.
5. Self-compassion: Resilient individuals show kindness and understanding towards themselves, acknowledging their own worth and value, and practicing self-care to maintain emotional well-being.

Chapter-12
Meaning

"The two most important days in your life are the day you are born and the day you find out why." - Mark Twain

In positive psychology, the concept of "meaning" refers to a deep sense of purpose, significance, and fulfillment in life. where individuals feel that their existence has value and their actions contribute to something greater than themselves. Meaning is derived from aligning one's activities with personal values, engaging in pursuits that bring fulfillment, and fostering connections with others.

✓ A nurse who finds deep meaning in her work may see her daily tasks not just as duties but as opportunities to alleviate suffering and bring comfort to patients.
✓ Similarly, a musician who creates music to inspire and uplift others may find meaning in the transformative power of art.
✓ Ultimately, meaning provides a sense of direction and coherence, guiding individuals to live authentically and make meaningful contributions to their own lives and the world around them.

"The purpose of life is not to be happy. It is to be useful, to be honorable, to be compassionate, to have it make some difference that you have lived and lived well." - Ralph Waldo Emerson

Your time is limited, so don't waste it living someone else's life. "~ Steve Jobs

Steve Jobs *was a visionary entrepreneur and technology innovator who co-founded Apple Inc., one of the most influential and successful companies in the world. Born on February 24, 1955, in San Francisco, California.Steve Jobs' personal life was marked by various struggles and challenges, many of which deeply influenced his growth and development as a person. One of the most profound struggles Jobs faced was his search for identity and belonging. Born to unwed parents and adopted shortly after birth, Jobs grappled with questions of identity throughout his life. He struggled with feelings of abandonment and the desire to connect with his biological family, a journey that he embarked on later in life.*

Jobs' unconventional personality and intense focus on his work often strained his relationships with family and friends. He was known for his perfectionism and demanding nature, which sometimes led to conflicts in his personal and professional life. Despite his successes, Jobs faced periods of loneliness and isolation, particularly during his early years at Apple when he was ousted from the company he co-founded.

Additionally, Jobs' health struggles were well-documented. In 2003, he was diagnosed with a rare form of pancreatic cancer, which he kept private for several years. He underwent surgery and treatment, but his health remained a concern throughout his life. Despite facing mortality, Jobs continued to lead Apple and pursue his vision with determination and resilience.

Jobs displayed an early interest in electronics and computers. He dropped out of college but continued his education by auditing classes that interested him, including calligraphy, which later influenced the typography of Apple's products.

"Stay hungry, stay foolish."

In 1976, Jobs, along with his friend Steve Wozniak and Ronald Wayne, founded Apple Computer, Inc. in the Jobs family garage. Their first product, the Apple I computer, was followed by the Apple II, which became a commercial success. However, it was the introduction of the Macintosh in 1984 that solidified Apple's reputation for innovation and design excellence.One of the most significant challenges Jobs faced was his ousting from Apple in 1985. After a power struggle with the company's board of directors, Jobs was removed from his position as the head of the Macintosh division. This event could have marked the end of his career, but instead, it fueled his determination to succeed on his own terms.

"Innovation distinguishes between a leader and a follower."

Undeterred, Jobs founded NeXT Inc., a computer platform development company, and Pixar Animation Studios. NeXT initially struggled to gain traction in the market, but Jobs remained committed to creating innovative products. Pixar, meanwhile, faced numerous financial challenges before finding success with groundbreaking animated films like "Toy Story."Jobs' ability to navigate failure and setbacks with resilience and determination is a testament to his character. He once said, "I'm convinced that about half of what separates the successful entrepreneurs from the non-successful ones is pure perseverance."

In 1997, Jobs returned to Apple when the company acquired NeXT. His second stint at Apple saw him spearhead the development of transformative products like the iMac, iTunes, iPod, iPhone, and iPad. These products not only revolutionized their respective industries but also cemented Apple's position as one of the most valuable and influential companies in the world.

Unlike a drop of water which loses its identity when it joins the ocean, man does not lose his being in the society in which he lives. Man's life is independent. He is born not for the development of the society alone, but for the development of his self. ~ Dr. B.R. Ambedkar

This quote by Dr. B.R. Ambedkar encapsulates the idea that individual identity and autonomy are essential aspects of human existence, distinct from the collective identity of society. Unlike a drop of water that loses its identity when it merges with the vastness of the ocean, a person does not lose their individuality when they become part of society.

Dr. Ambedkar emphasizes that while humans are social beings and live within societies, their lives are not solely defined by their roles within those societies. Instead, each person has an inherent independence and purpose in life that goes beyond serving the needs of society alone.The quote underscores the importance of self-development and self-realization as fundamental aspects of human existence. According to Dr. Ambedkar, individuals are born not only to contribute to the progress and well-being of society but also to cultivate their own *growth, fulfillment, and potential.Overall, this quote encourages individuals to recognize their intrinsic value and agency, highlighting the significance of personal development and autonomy in shaping one's life journey.*

The importance of meaning in life as the foundational element of human development. Just as a building needs a sturdy foundation to stand tall and withstand challenges, individuals require a sense of purpose and meaning to navigate life's complexities and thrive.

Meaning in life provides a guiding light, shaping individuals' beliefs, values, and goals. Without it, life can feel directionless and devoid of fulfillment, much like a building without a solid foundation.Moreover, much like the quality of the bricks used in construction impacts the strength and resilience of a building, the quality of the meaning individuals find in their lives influences the depth and robustness of their personal development. A profound sense of meaning empowers individuals to overcome obstacles, pursue their passions, and contribute to the world around them.

Chapter-13

Accomplishment or Mastery or Competence

"Success is not final, failure is not fatal: It is the courage to continue that counts." - Winston Churchill

Feeling accomplished happens when you work hard to achieve your goals, get good at something, and stay determined to finish what you started. This makes you feel proud of yourself and happy with your life.

Accomplishment means not giving up and loving what you do. But true happiness and feeling good come when you work towards things because you really want to, not just because you have to or for external rewards.When you focus on personal growth and building relationships, it makes you feel even better than chasing after things like money or fame. It's about finding joy in the journey and improving yourself from within

Need for Accomplishment

Need of accomplishment wanting to do important things, become really good at something, be in charge, or have high standards.McClelland studied this and found that people with a strong need for achievement have certain traits:

- Moderate risk propensity;
- Undertaking innovative and engaging tasks;
- Internal locus of control and responsibility for own decisions and behaviors;
- Need for precise goal setting.

In 1982, McClelland and others did a study.

They found that people with a high need for achievement did well in jobs where they could show their individual skills and get promoted based on that. But in jobs where leadership was more important for promotion, having a high need for achievement didn't always lead to success.

Subedar Major Neeraj Chopra PVSM VSM is indeed an Indian track and field athlete who has made history in javelin throw. He is the reigning Olympic champion and World champion in men's javelin throw. Neeraj Chopra made history by becoming the first Asian athlete to win an Olympic gold medal in javelin throw at the Tokyo 2020 Olympics. Additionally, he became the first Asian to win gold in his event at the World Championships. His remarkable achievements have not only brought pride to India but have also cemented his legacy as one of the greatest javelin throwers in the world. Vince Lobardi has quoted "The greatest accomplishment is not in never falling, but in rising again after you fall."This will perfectly opt for Neeraj.

Neeraj Chopra, an Indian javelin thrower, believes that his failures have played a big role in making him the successful athlete he is today. He mentioned that he started competing internationally in 2017 but faced many losses until 2021. It was only in 2022 that he finally achieved success by getting a podium position in the Diamond League.In 2019, Chopra had to miss the whole season because of an injury to his right elbow. After undergoing surgery, he couldn't play for over six months. However, he went to South Africa to train under a biomechanics expert named Klaus Bartoneitz.

Chopra's journey reached its peak when he won the gold medal at the Tokyo 2020 Olympics. Despite missing the Commonwealth Games in 2022 due to another injury, he became the first Indian world champion in athletics by winning the men's javelin throw gold at Budapest 2023. He also won gold at the Hangzhou Asian Games that year.Even with all these successes, Chopra stays humble. He believes that accepting defeats as a normal part of sports has helped him stay grounded amidst his winning streak.

"Success is not the key to happiness. Happiness is the key to success. If you love what you are doing, you will be successful." - Albert Schweitzer

Ways to build a sense of accomplishment:

"Believe you can and you're halfway there." - Theodore Roosevelt

Virat Kohli, one of cricket's greatest, has inspired many with his talent and resilience. When he was just 18, playing for Delhi, his father passed away suddenly. Despite this huge loss, Kohli showed incredible strength by deciding to play a crucial match the same day. He honored his father's wishes, prioritizing cricket, and went on to score a remarkable 90 runs, saving the match alongside his teammate Punit Bisht. Kohli later revealed that his father's dream was for him to play for India, which became his driving force. This determination earned him respect from his teammates and fans. Kohli's ability to overcome personal tragedy and excel on the field showcases his mental toughness and dedication to the sport. Since then, he has continued to thrive, cementing his status as a cricket legend.

Set SMART Goals: Make goals that are Specific, Measurable, Achievable, Realistic, and Time-bound. This helps you stay focused and gives you a clear path to success.

Reflect on Past Successes: Take time to think about times when you've succeeded before. Remembering your past accomplishments can boost your confidence and motivation.

Celebrate Achievements Creatively: Find fun and creative ways to celebrate when you reach your goals, no matter how big or small they are. It could be treating yourself to something you enjoy, sharing your success with friends or family, or simply taking a moment to acknowledge your hard work.

By setting clear goals, remembering your past successes, and celebrating your achievements, you can build a strong sense of accomplishment and satisfaction in your life.

Chapter-14

Gratitude

"Gratitude is the healthiest of all human emotions. The more you express gratitude for what you have, the more likely you will have even more to express gratitude for."
- Zig Ziglar

Gratitude is the quality of being thankful and appreciative for the good things in one's life. It involves recognizing and acknowledging the blessings, kindness, and positive experiences that one receives from others, as well as from life in general. Gratitude goes beyond mere politeness or saying "thank you"; it's a deeper, heartfelt appreciation for what one has, whether it's tangible or intangible. Cultivating gratitude can lead to increased happiness, resilience, and overall well-being. It involves focusing on what one has rather than what one lacks, and it can foster positive relationships, improve mental health, and contribute to a more fulfilling life.

"Gratitude is when memory is stored in the heart and not in the mind." - Lionel Hampton

Gratitude of TATA - SUMO

The Tata Sumo is a popular vehicle made by Tata Motors, a leading car manufacturer in India. The name has nothing to do with Japanese sumo wrestlers.

*Every day, the top executives of Tata Motors had lunch together, but Mr. Sumant Moolgaokar often disappeared during lunch break and returned after a long time. So where he is taking his lunch ? One day, it has been surprisely observed that, he his taking lunch simple roadside eatery (dhaba***), talking to truck drivers*** and taking notes on their feedback about Tata vehicles. He is not taking any fifestar hotel lunch. He used this feedback to suggest improvements to the Tata design and R&D teams.*

To honor his dedication and unique way of working, Tata Motors named their first multi-utility vehicle "Tata Sumo"—combining the first parts of his name, "Su" from Sumant and "Mo" from Moolgaokar. The name "Tata Sumo" is a tribute to Sumant Moolgaokar, who was the Managing Director of Tata Motors. Unlike what some might think

Sumant Moolgaokar passed away in July 1989. His contributions are still celebrated today by Tata employees, showing how deeply they respected and valued his work.

In psychology, gratitude is studied as a positive emotion and a personality trait that contributes to overall well-being and mental health. Research in positive psychology has shown that practicing gratitude can lead to numerous psychological benefits. Gratitude is associated with increased happiness, life satisfaction, and positive mood. When individuals express gratitude, whether through journaling, reflecting, or expressing thanks to others, they tend to experience greater levels of subjective well-being.Furthermore, gratitude is linked to improved relationships and social connections. Expressing gratitude towards others strengthens interpersonal bonds, fosters empathy, and promotes prosocial behavior. In turn, these positive relationships contribute to greater psychological resilience and overall satisfaction with life.

Gratitude also plays a role in coping with adversity and stress. Individuals who regularly practice gratitude tend to exhibit greater resilience in the face of challenges. By focusing on what they are thankful for, even during difficult times, they can maintain a more positive outlook and cope more effectively with stressors.Moreover, research suggests that gratitude is associated with physical health benefits, such as better sleep, reduced symptoms of depression and anxiety, and lower levels of stress hormones.

Gratitude is like the Tip of an Iceberg

Gratitude, much like the tip of an iceberg, represents only a small visible portion of a much larger whole. When we think of gratitude, we often focus on the significant and overt blessings in our lives—things like family, health, and success. These are the "tip" of our gratitude iceberg, readily apparent and easily recognized.

However, beneath the surface lies a vast expanse of experiences and moments for which we can also be grateful. These are the everyday occurrences, the simple pleasures, and the fleeting moments of joy that may often go unnoticed or underappreciated. They make up the bulk of our gratitude iceberg, representing the deeper layers of our appreciation.Just as the submerged portion of an iceberg constitutes the majority of its mass, so too do these everyday blessings constitute the majority of our opportunities for gratitude. Whether it's the warmth of a morning cup of coffee, the beauty of a sunset, or the comfort of a familiar song, these small moments enrich our lives in meaningful ways.

By expanding our awareness to include these subtler aspects of gratitude, we deepen our practice and cultivate a richer sense of appreciation for the world around us. Like exploring the depths of the ocean to discover hidden treasures, delving into the depths of our gratitude allows us to uncover a wealth of blessings that may have otherwise gone unnoticed.So, while the tip of the iceberg may catch our attention with its grandeur, it is the vastness beneath the surface that truly sustains us and enriches our lives. Let us embrace the full spectrum of gratitude, from the towering peaks to the depths below, and find abundance in every moment.

"Gratitude is the fairest blossom which springs from the soul." - Henry Ward Beecher

Chapter-15

Hope

Hope is being able to see that there is light despite all of the darkness." - Desmond Tutu

Hope is considered a fundamental component of psychological well-being and plays a crucial role in fostering positive outcomes in various aspects of life, including mental health, relationships, and achievement.Research in positive psychology suggests that individuals with high levels of hope tend to experience greater overall happiness, satisfaction, and life fulfillment. They are better equipped to cope with stress, setbacks, and disappointments, as they maintain a positive outlook and focus on solutions rather than problems.

Don't think about the start of the race. Think about the ending." Usain Bolt

Usain Bolt set world records in both the 100 meters (9.58 seconds) and the 200 meters (19.19 seconds) at the 2009 World Championships in Berlin. Additionally, he's part of the Jamaican 4x100 meters relay team that holds the world record.Bolt's incredible speed and track dominance earned him the nickname "Lightning Bolt" and the title of the "fastest man alive" during his career.What is the hope of investment, Usain Bold has won 9 gold medals in last 3 Olympics and has run less than 2 minutes on the track.

Usain Bolt ran for less than 115 seconds in total in his Olympic and made USD 119 Million. That's more *than USD1 Million for each second he ran. But for those 115 seconds, he trained himself for 20 + years. That's hope of progress he is firm beliver of* **"I know what I can do, so I never doubt myself."***It is not so easy to him to achieve, When he was 17 years old, doctors told him he had scoliosis. This meant his spine was bent because he grew too fast and trained too hard. He had to deal with this problem for a long time.then he decided* **"Dreams are free. Goals have a cost. While you can daydream for free, goals don't come without a price. Time, Effort, Sac rifice, and Sweat. How will you pay for your goals?"**

During the Athens Olympics in 2004, Usain wanted to win gold, but he couldn't. After running the first 200 meters, he felt pain in his thigh. Sadly, he had to go back home to Jamaica without achieving his dream.
In the 2005 World Championships in Helsinki, Usain didn't do as well as he hoped. His health wasn't good, and he didn't perform his best, finishing with a time of 26.27 seconds.
A hamstring injury stopped Usain from participating in the 2006 Commonwealth Games.Despite these challenges, Usain stays focused on his goals. He knows what it takes to be a champion, so he keeps working hard to achieve his dreams. He have strong hope **" "Worrying gets you nowhere. If you turn up worrying about how you're going to perform, you've already lost. Train hard, turn up, run your best, and the rest will take care of itself."**

In positive psychology, hope is a powerful concept that refers to the belief that one can achieve their goals, even in the face of adversity or challenges. It is characterized by a sense of optimism, resilience, and determination to pursue one's aspirations, regardless of obstacles that may arise.

Once all villgers decided to pray for rain. On the day of prayer all people gathered but only one boy came with an Umbrella.

Hopeful individuals are more likely to set and work towards meaningful goals, persist in the face of challenges, and adapt to changing circumstances. They possess a sense of agency and belief in their own abilities, which empowers them to take proactive steps towards realizing their aspirations.

When you toss a one year old baby in the air, he laughs because heknows his father will catch him.

Hope is contagious and can have ripple effects on others. Individuals who exude hopefulness inspire and motivate those around them, creating a supportive and optimistic environment conducive to growth and success.

Every night we go to bed, we have no assurance to wakeup alive next morning,but still we set alarm for tomorrow.

Practicing hope in daily life involves cultivating a mindset of possibility, reframing setbacks as opportunities for learning and growth, and maintaining a sense of purpose and direction. This may include setting realistic goals, visualizing success, seeking support from others, and taking consistent action towards desired outcomes.

**_"When the world says 'give up,' hope whispers,
'try one more time.'" – Unknown_**

In a quiet room, four candles were burning slowly. They flickered softly, almost like they were talking. Their words sounded sad...The first candle said, "I am Peace, but these days, nobody wants to keep me burning." Then its flame got smaller and smaller until it went out completely.

The second candle said, "I am Faith, but these days, I am not needed anymore." Then its flame also faded away and disappeared.Sadly, the third candle spoke up, "I am Love, but I don't have the strength to stay lit anymore. People don't understand how important I am. They forget to love those close to them." And then, Love's flame went out too.

Suddenly, a child walked into the room and saw the three candles that had stopped burning. The child started crying, "Why aren't you burning? You're supposed to stay lit until the end. What will I do without peace, faith, and love?"Then, the fourth candle spoke gently to the child, "Don't be scared, because I am Hope. As long as I'm still burning, we can light the other candles again. Let's do it together."

With excitement, the child took the Candle of Hope and used it to relight the other three candles. Sometimes, you might see them flicker and go out again. But as long as Hope keeps shining, the other three will always be there for us.

_"Hope is the only thing stronger than fear." - Suzanne
Collins_